The Digital Principal

*How to encourage a technology-rich learning environment
that meets the needs of teachers and students*

JANETTE HUGHES

ANNE BURKE

Pembroke Publishers Limited

For Timothy, Alexander, and Molly — my digital learners
— Janette Hughes

For my digikids Aidan, Lily, and Bella
— Anne Burke

© 2014 Pembroke Publishers
538 Hood Road
Markham, Ontario, Canada L3R 3K9
www.pembrokepublishers.com

Distributed in the U.S. by Stenhouse Publishers
480 Congress Street
Portland, ME 04101
www.stenhouse.com

We acknowledge the financial support of the Government of Canada through the Canada Book Fund (CBF) for our publishing activities.

We acknowledge the assistance of the Government of Ontario through the Ontario Media Development Corporation's Ontario Book Initiative.

Library and Archives Canada Cataloguing in Publication

Hughes, Janette, author
    The digital principal / Janette Hughes, Anne Burke.

Includes bibliographical references and index.
Issued in print and electronic formats.
ISBN 978-1-55138-288-3 (pbk.).--ISBN 978-1-55138-854-0 (pdf)

    1. Educational leadership. 2. Educational innovations. 3. Educational technology.
4. Education--Data processing. 5. Internet in education. 6. Mass media in education.
I. Burke, Anne M. (Anne Michelle), author II. Title.

LB2806.H85 2013   371.2   C2013-904233-4
                                        C2013-904234-2

Editor: Kate Revingon
Cover Design: John Zehethofer
Typesetting: Jay Tee Graphics Ltd.

Printed and bound in Canada
9 8 7 6 5 4 3 2 1

MIX
Paper from
responsible sources
FSC® C004071

Contents

1

Embracing Technology Through Transformational Leadership

As you know, we live in an information society in which many of us use digital technologies, such as the Internet, mobile devices, and video, every day. We search for and obtain information for reasons such as shopping, holiday research, and personal interest, and we socialize with one another. Reigeluth and Karnopp (2013) argue that key characteristics of the Information Age are contributing to fundamental shifts in society. These characteristics include "customization, diversity, collaboration, team-based organizational structures, shared leadership, empowerment with accountability, initiative or self-direction, self-service, and holism or systems thinking" (p. 21). Given the time we spend using digital technologies in our personal lives, we as educators must address our students' need to learn how to use — and benefit from — these tools — specifically, the computer and the Internet. Indeed, becoming digitally literate can be seen as a key life skill for success.

So, if we accept the premise that digital technologies have already changed the ways we live and interact with one another, it follows that we should embrace the use of technology in schools, while ensuring that students use it critically and strategically. The importance of this endeavor cannot be overstated. Michael Fullan (1993), educational leadership and change expert, argues, "Technology has dramatically affected virtually every sector in society that you can think of *except* education" (p. 72). In other words, technological change is driving society in innovative ways, but schools have been less inclined to explore the use of technology as a pedagogical tool.

Why Our Students Need to Learn with Technology

We are at a crossroads — a critical moment in which we can choose to help students deal with the potential, promise, and challenges of digital technologies, or not. The invention of Gutenberg's printing press in 1450 had a huge impact on the oral tradition, and the commercialization of television in the 1950s changed our relationship with media. So, too, the emergence of digital technologies profoundly affects how we engage with information and how we express ourselves. We live in a participatory culture — a few short years ago, the Internet was primarily a source of information delivered to the user in one direction. Now anyone can contribute to the content found online. Access to the Internet and to mobile devices is becoming cheaper and easier, and every year, more of our students become anytime-anywhere users of digital tools of all kinds. We need to attend to this shift in our schools, and the time to take action is now.

As educators, we need to establish learning environments that engage students in a variety of modalities for learning that are relevant to their experiences outside school. A 2009 report of the Canadian Council on Learning, *Post-secondary Education in Canada: Meeting Our Needs?*, observes, "Rapid technological change, global competitive pressures and new patterns of work are demanding a more sophisticated set of transferable skills, such as problem-solving, communication, decision-making, teamwork, leadership, entrepreneurship and adaptability" (p. 58). If we do not engage our students in learning with technology, we risk not preparing them to meet the numerous challenges of the future.

What research says about technology integration

Beyond that, research is establishing that learning with technology brings benefits. Anyone who has witnessed first-hand the power of technology to engage and motivate students knows that technology integration can have a positive impact on student learning. As educational researchers, we have been working with students of all ages in schools, and we have found that students are more engaged and motivated when using new technologies, but also that they make gains in terms of developing the digital literacies skills they need to succeed academically (Burke, Hughes, Hardware, & Thompson, 2013; Hughes, Thompson, & Burke, 2013).

Our research investigates how teachers and students use digital tools of all kinds to explore issues of self and community identities, and develop digital literacies skills while doing so. We have found that students, when given opportunities to use digital tools to explore curriculum content, not only become proficient users of a variety of the tools, but also develop collaborative and communication skills while engaging in small-group problem solving and decision making. They are required to synthesize multiple streams of simultaneous modes and information while reading and producing digital texts. They also learn to critique, analyze, and evaluate multimedia texts, such as websites, videos, photo essays, and graphic texts, including comic strips and graphic novels. The students learn about the responsibilities of digital citizenship that go hand in hand with using technology, but more important, they learn about the power of digital media to convey important messages related to social justice issues and how they can effect change by creating awareness and taking action within their communities. This inquiry-based approach integrates technology with discipline-specific content and interdisciplinary skills, such as critical thinking, research skills, and information literacy skills.

In their 2000 report for the Software & Information Industry Association, Sivin-Kachala and Bialo confirm this. They note that, when students use computers for learning, they feel successful and motivated, and they show increased self-confidence and self-esteem; they also make academic gains. Further, the report indicates that students involved in small-group collaborative learning while using a computer achieved more than students using the computer alone or independently. This report was based on 311 research reviews and reports that focused on original research.

The International Society for Technology in Education (ISTE) and the Center for Applied Research in Educational Technology (CARET) conducted a review of research, as well. The authors (Cradler, McNabb, Freeman, and Burchett) of the 2002 report "How Does Technology Influence Student Learning?" identify the following benefits of technology integration:

> "In the end, the students themselves demonstrate whether technology use is effectively embedded in their learning. Effective use of technology can improve student engagement. Student engagement increases when students are interested in the task at hand and have the tools they need to accomplish it. Engaged students focus on the task rather than the tool. The result is improved student achievement. That is the most important and final marker."
> — Principal Jill Foster

At the heart of our endeavor is this question: "How can we best use digital media to enhance student learning?"

To read the Executive Summary, go to http://www.siia.net/estore/REF-00-summary.pdf.

- improved student achievement in reading, writing, and mathematics, according to standardized tests in the United States
- improved attendance, decreased dropout rates, and increased graduation rates
- increased parental involvement
- improved learning skills, particularly thinking skills, problem-solving skills, information and communication skills
- improved workforce skills

Check out http://www.edutopia.org/technology-integration.

So, whether to help better prepare students to deal with a dauntingly digital world or to exploit the potential of digital technologies for learning, schools have a responsibility to address digital technologies and their role in education. Doing that begins with the principal.

The call for a digital principal

This book will not teach you everything you need to know about current technologies and how to use them — digital tools are emerging too rapidly for us to keep up with the latest trendy tool. In any event, that is not the kind of information your students need from school. Instead, we offer an *approach* or *orientation* to technology not dependent on your experience with or knowledge of specific digital tools. With this approach, you will be well able to create and promote a climate of innovation, to support your teachers as they use digital tools to enhance teaching and learning, to stay abreast of current research related to technology in education, and to manage digital innovation in the school as new technologies emerge and have an impact on how students learn.

As an educational leader, you may be called on to encourage a culture of technological innovation in your school or to create an effective school technology plan. These require an attitude or approach more than any level of technological knowledge. As a digital principal, you can apply your existing leadership skills to the challenge of creating and supporting a learning environment rich in technology. By *digital principal*, we mean an educational leader who is intent on maximizing student learning through the effective infusion of digital technologies. You do not need to know the intricate details of how the technology works; however, we do encourage you to position yourself as a learner alongside the teachers, staff, and students in your school.

In this resource, we promote and encourage a *transformational leadership* style that, we believe, is critical to facilitating successful implementation of technology in schools. This approach emphasizes that all stakeholders must have input into decisions, including the development of a shared vision for technology initiatives. Involving all stakeholders — teachers, students, families, and administrative staff — will help ensure the most accurate and authoritative understanding of how to meet students' technology-related needs. The standards of the International Society for Technology in Education (ISTE), which we strongly support, set a standard of excellence and best practices in learning, teaching, and leading with technology in schools and point to the value of an educational administrator having a transformational leadership style. The digital principal is a transformational school leader.

Leading and Learning Together — Transformational Leadership

Kenneth Leithwood, author of more than 10 books on educational leadership, has led research on transformational leadership since the early 1990s. In his seminal article, "The Move Toward Transformational Leadership," he argued that transformational school leaders are in continuous pursuit of three fundamental goals:

1) helping staff members develop and maintain a collaborative, professional school culture;
2) fostering teacher development; and
3) helping them solve problems together more effectively.
(Leithwood, 1992, 9–10)

In his subsequent research and the research of others, such as Bass and Avolio, four elements of transformational leadership were identified: (1) idealized influence, (2) inspirational motivation, (3) intellectual stimulation, and (4) individualized consideration (Bass & Avolio, 1994). These are outlined below.

1. *Idealized influence* refers to how well the leader acts as a role model for others. Transformational leaders "walk the talk" and embody the values that they espouse so that followers will learn the same behaviors and, in turn, model for others, who may adopt those behaviors, too. A foundational principle of transformational leadership is the promotion of a consistent vision, something that provides followers with meaningful purpose. Transformational leaders work persistently, enthusiastically, and optimistically to foster a collaborative environment of teamwork and commitment.
2. *Inspirational motivation* refers to how well the leader articulates a vision that inspires others and compels them to follow. Transformational leaders paint a picture for followers to show them where they are going; they thereby provide them with motivation to act. They challenge followers to take risks. Leaders with inspirational motivation can communicate goals in ways that make the vision clear, powerful, and engaging. As a result, followers feel encouraged and positive about the future — more willing to buy-in to any innovation or change.
3. *Intellectual stimulation* refers to how well the leader stirs the imaginations of followers through encouragement and support of innovation and creativity. Transformational leaders encourage their followers to think creatively, and they do not penalize them or criticize them for mistakes. They focus on resolving problems productively and are more likely to try something new and untested than to rely on traditional, accepted practices that seem not to be working.
4. *Individualized consideration* refers to how well the leader attends to each follower's needs, acts as a mentor or coach to the follower, and listens to the concerns and needs of the follower. Transformational leaders provide support, stand alongside followers, treat people as individuals, and respect their contributions to the team. This approach, in turn, develops intrinsic motivation in followers.

Each of these elements is founded on the respect, integrity, encouragement, and influence that are part of transformational leadership. The transformational

You could say that this community approach taps into Web 2.0 affordances, the bringing together of collective intelligence being one thing that digital technologies enable. See "Leadership that draws on Web 2.0 affordances," below, for more on affordances.

leader must be genuine and transparent in order to create the kind of trust necessary for change and innovation to occur. Transformational leaders are change-savvy, but also seek to have followers become leaders exercising autonomy.

Transformational leadership focuses on empowering stakeholders — particularly teachers — to participate in decision making, problem solving, and innovation. It relies on a community approach: one that emphasizes the bringing together of collective intelligence, collaboration, and the overall knowledge of the community. The community learns and leads together, under the guidance and support of the principal.

Although not obliged to be a tech expert to meet the demands of the digital school, you *do* need a collaborative approach to leadership. You will be required to mentor, motivate, inspire, encourage, facilitate, and support the people in your school community. In your leadership toolbox, you will already have the ability to communicate effectively, and you will need to draw on this to ensure that everyone is striving to meet your school's common goals. So, far from meaning that a school is leaderless, transformational leadership supports a team approach and a sharing of leadership roles with others.

The need to share ideas and expertise

New technologies are constantly emerging, so making appropriate decisions for your school may feel like trying to hit a moving target. For example, only a few years ago, many school districts were aiming to put three or four networked computers in every classroom; now, with the growing popularity of tablets and other mobile devices, school districts are rethinking their strategies. Some are even moving to a Bring Your Own Device (BYOD) model. The digital classroom cannot be mediated by one person reflecting the traditional notion of leadership.

To deal with the rapidity of technological advancements, educational leadership must be increasingly decentralized, as in transformational leadership. Decentralization of educational leadership is defined through shared expertise: classroom teachers may have to defer to their students for best practices in using new technologies, and the most digitally fluent staff are, of course, better suited to lead digital instruction, such as that pertaining to sharing of resources, differentiation, and co-teaching initiatives.

"Democratisation of educational systems is a logical replacement to centralized authoritative organisational structures."
— Franciosi, 2012, p. 243

When it comes to technology, we cannot tell with certainty what will emerge next and how it will have an impact on education; however, what seems certain is that engaging more voices in the discussion will improve how we integrate technology with education.

Leadership that draws on Web 2.0 affordances

A Long Way from 1.0 to 2.0

The term *Web 2.0* is generally accredited to Tim O'Reilly following a 2004 conference dealing with next-generation Web concepts and issues; however, Joe Firmage used *Web 2.0* to describe using the World Wide Web as a platform even earlier, in 2003. *Web 2.0* signifies the greatly increased interactivity of the Web, which has gone from being a read-only tool to becoming the ReadWrite Web that enables collective and collaborative participation.

One significant difference between Web 2.0 and the traditional World Wide Web — or Web 1.0, as it has been retroactively called — is greater collaboration among Internet users and other users, content providers, and enterprises. Formerly, it was most common to post data on websites and have users view or download the content. Increasingly, users have far more input into the nature and scope of Web content — in some cases, they exert real-time control over it. Notions of authority and expertise shift in a Web 2.0 paradigm where anyone who is knowledgeable about a subject (and even someone who is not!) can post information on a blog or website. This shift facilitates an approach that values distributed, or shared, leadership; greater interactivity among users permits and encourages the development of transformational leadership — it also raises the matter of affordances versus constraints.

The term *affordances* has been applied by researchers in the area of information and communication technologies (ICTs) and digital literacies to the evaluation of digital tools (see, for example, Kennewell, 2001). Jones and Hafner (2012) use the term in association with Marshall McLuhan's assertion that, while new technologies "extend certain parts of us, they amputate other parts" (p. 3). In our book, the term *affordances* refers to the actions, attributes, or characteristics of a digital tool that allow a user to create and participate; the term *constraints* is used to describe the limitations placed on the user as a result of choosing a particular digital tool. For example, social networking sites enable, or afford, the user to communicate with a global audience; at the same time, they may put a student at risk of exposing too many personal details in a public forum. Some affordances of digital tools that we highlight are accessibility, communication, collaboration, immediacy, and multimodality.

Affordances, a term coined by J. J. Gibson in 1977, refers to what an environment or an object enables people or animals within that environment to perform for good or ill. For example, a doorknob *affords* the user an opportunity to open a door.

Roles of the transformational leader

As noted above, transformational leaders in education act as positive role models who motivate other community members to act for common purpose; they also encourage risk taking. In a sense, the digital principal is a leader among leaders: a kind of coordinator, facilitator, and cheerleader.

When it comes to coordinating, a transformational leader fulfills three key roles: (1) motivator, (2) communicator, and (3) facilitator of communication. As *motivator*, the leader inspires school community members to work together towards meeting the school's goals. In order to succeed in this role, the digital principal must understand the goals and the situated context of the community — student population, history, location, size, and so on. As *communicator*, the transformational leader periodically reminds community members of the school's goals and overall vision. The third role — that of *facilitator* of communication — is also important. Franciosi (2012) notes that in an environment where risk taking and experimenting are valued, the ability to learn from mistakes is "the key to efficiency." Since no one can learn from the experiences of another if unaware of what someone has done, "it falls to the leader to ensure that adequate and productive communication takes place" (n.p.).

Getting Past Words to Action

As in all areas of education, the terminology surrounding technology and education shifts and evolves. We could talk about information and communication technologies (ICTs), educational technology, or technology in education, or we could use the term *technology integration* or maybe *technology infusion*.

There will always be someone who argues that one term is better than another. For some people, the term *technology integration* implies that technology is an add-on or frill incorporated into the existing or traditional educational context when notions of teaching and learning should be radicalized. Similarly, for others, the term *technology infusion* suggests that the existing system or environment needs some kind of injection to prevent it from ailing. As for us, we prefer the term *digital literacies* (which is defined in the next section).

Ultimately, the terms matter less than what we do with technology in our schools.

So, What Does It Mean to Be *Digitally Literate?*

Digital citizenship is the subject of Chapter 6.

Although issues pertaining to equal access persist, technology in schools has become commonplace. Most, if not all, district school boards across North America have technology strategic plans that school administrators are required to implement. To be an effective instructional leader in this area, an administrator needs to know what it means to be "digitally literate."

At time of writing, we found at least 20 different definitions of the term *digital literacies*, but most of these definitions focus on a person's ability to use technological tools. For us, *digital literacies* goes beyond proficiency with the tools of technology. We view digital literacies as social practice: it encompasses being able to collaborate and communicate in particular contexts while solving problems and making decisions; being able to synthesize multiple streams of simultaneous modes and information during reading and producing; being able to critique, analyze, and evaluate multimedia texts; and, of course, being good digital citizens.

To put it more succinctly, in order to be digitally literate, our students need to be users, critics, and producers of digital texts and information (Selber, 2004). They need to have the skills and knowledge to use a variety of digital media software applications and hardware devices; to be able to critically understand digital media content and applications; and to possess the knowledge and capacity to create with digital technologies. Indeed, we want our students not merely to consume digital texts, but to be able to produce them to meet particular purposes and needs. Furthermore, while being literate has traditionally meant the ability to read and write, which certainly involves cognitive processes, in digital literacies, interpersonal and social processes are also recognized as essential elements.

Belshaw's e-book is available at http://dougbelshaw.com/blog/2014/01/06/essential-elements-v09/.

The figure below, adapted from Doug Belshaw's (2014) e-book, *The Essential Elements of Digital Literacies,* depicts the various elements of digital literacies. As the figure suggests, it is better for us to focus on how the tools provide users with affordances, such as communicating, connecting, creating, thinking critically, constructing new knowledge, and moving towards civic engagement and social action, than to focus on the digital tools themselves.

The standards of the International Society for Technology in Education

The International Society for Technology in Education (ISTE) represents more than 100 000 educators and education leaders seeking to improve learning and teaching through furthering effective use of technology in education by students and teachers. Beyond fulfilling its role to help people worldwide understand how, when, and for what purpose to use various technologies, the International Society for Technology in Education has developed global standards for administrators, for teachers, for students, and for technology coaches. These standards represent a type of road map that educators can use to leverage digital technologies: the goal is to make learning more relevant, productive, equitable, and efficient than it has traditionally been for students.

In terms of student learning, it is relevant to note the categories that the International Society for Technology in Education has identified as important:

- creativity and innovation
- communication and collaboration
- research and information fluency
- critical thinking, problem solving, and decision making
- digital citizenship

You can see that the focus is *not* on how to use digital tools. The specific digital tools used will continue to emerge, evolve, trend — and fade; and the ways in which they are used will shift accordingly. While we want our students to be able to use digital technologies effectively — that is, to choose appropriate tools for appropriate purposes — the ISTE categories emphasize that students be able to create, communicate, collaborate, connect, think critically, and act as good digital citizens.

Despite changes in the technologies, the conditions necessary to facilitate their effective use for teaching and learning remain constant. These are outlined below.

Conditions Required for the Effective School Use of Technologies

"Essential Conditions: Necessary Conditions to Effectively Leverage Technology for Learning" appears on the ISTE website: http://www.iste.org/docs/pdfs/netsessentialconditions.pdf?sfvrsn=2.

SEE CHAPTER 2.

The International Society for Technology in Education has identified 14 conditions that must be present if a school is to use digital technologies effectively to enhance student learning. As you review each condition outlined, consider how well your school satisfies it. Marginal notations indicate where in this book we discuss each condition, including advice on how to achieve it.

1. Shared Vision

Education stakeholders — teachers and support staff, school and district administrators, teacher-educators, students, parents, and community members among them — share a vision for the use of technology in the school, as a result of a leadership initiative. This vision must be negotiated and co-constructed, rather than imposed on the community from the top down. Although it can originate from school leaders, the digital principal requires the support of the community to move forward.

SEE CHAPTER 2.

2. Empowered Leaders

All kinds of stakeholders are leaders focused on achieving desired change in the way that digital resources are employed. The transformational leader, committed to a shared leadership model, encourages all stakeholders to take part in the decision-making process.

SEE CHAPTER 2.

3. Planning for Implementation

A whole-school plan that reflects a vision that the school community shares addresses how to promote school effectiveness and student learning through the infusion of ICT and digital learning resources. The digital principal encourages active participation from the school community in every step of the planning and implementation phases.

SEE CHAPTER 5.

4. Consistent and Adequate Funding

Funding provides appropriate support for technology infrastructure, personnel, digital resources, and staff development. The digital principal ensures that the community has the resources it needs in order to succeed before expecting innovation and change to occur. Anything short of this sets people up for failure.

SEE CHAPTERS 3 AND 6.

5. Equitable Access

All students, teachers, staff, and school leaders enjoy reliable access to technologies and digital resources, both current and emerging. The digital principal ensures that decisions about technology allocation are reasonable and fair, and based on individual contexts and cases.

SEE CHAPTERS 4 AND 5.

6. Skilled Personnel

Because transformational leaders work to identify and promote leadership skills in others, they need to be selective when hiring and when making decisions about professional development. Digital principals are skilled in choosing and effectively using appropriate ICT resources.

SEE CHAPTER 4.

7. Ongoing Professional Learning

Educators have focused time to learn about and share ideas related to digital literacies. The digital principal ensures that related plans for professional learning are developed and implemented.

SEE CHAPTER 5.

8. Technical Support

Help in maintaining, renewing, and using ICT and digital learning resources is consistent and reliable. The digital principal ensures that community members have access to technical support, both from internal and external sources — teachers cannot be asked to innovate and then be left to founder.

SEE CHAPTER 3.

9. Enhanced Curriculum Framework

Content standards and related digital curriculum resources support digital-age learning and work appropriately. Teachers need opportunities to explore how different digital tools best fit into curricular areas and how these tools might enhance existing curriculum by infusing more technology.

SEE CHAPTER 3.

10. Student-Centered Learning

Planning, teaching, and assessment are all based on students' needs and abilities. A technology-rich environment best suits an inquiry approach to learning, in which students use digital tools to enhance their experiences in the classroom.

SEE CHAPTER 5.

11. Valuing of Assessment and Evaluation

Assessment of how technology can help in teaching, learning, and leadership is continuous; evaluation of how ICT and digital resources are used is ongoing. A school's recognition of their vitality within the community is a part of this process. Self and peer evaluation, along with established standards of measurement, or metrics, help determine how initiatives are progressing.

SEE CHAPTERS 2 AND 6.

12. Engaged Communities

Within communities, partnerships flourish, and collaboration is evident in the effort to support and fund the use of ICT and digital learning resources. The digital principal encourages all members of the school community, including parents, and other school stakeholders, such as community partners, to participate in planning, implementing, and evaluating.

SEE CHAPTERS 2 AND 5.

13. Policies for Support

Policies, financial plans, accountability measures, and incentive structures serve to support the use of digital resources for learning and in district school operations. The digital principal is familiar with policies and procedures at the local school and school district levels and beyond.

SEE CHAPTERS 4 AND 5.

14. Supportive External Context

Policies and initiatives at all levels, including regional and local, support schools and teacher preparation programs in how to effectively implement technology in order to enhance student learning.

More detail about ISTE Standards for Administrators can be found here: http://www.iste.org/standards/standards-for-administrators.

Key Themes for the Digital Principal

As indicated earlier, the International Society for Technology in Education has published standards for evaluating the skills and knowledge that educational administrators need in order to integrate technology and implement systemic reform in schools. ISTE Standards for Administrators address these five themes:

- visionary leadership
- digital-age learning culture
- excellence in professional practice
- systemic improvement
- digital citizenship

We have based the remaining chapters of this book on those themes, as they point to specific goals for educational leaders to strive to attain. We hope that, mastery of technological tools aside, you will gain a viable and practical approach to achieving systemic reform. You will play an instrumental role in leveraging the potential of technology in education for the students of your school. You will come to exemplify transformational leadership.

2

Visionary Leadership

The digital principal is the spark that ignites a shared vision for how technology will be integrated into the school in a comprehensive way. The digital principal guides the evolution and realization of a vision that can support transformation of the school into a dynamic, interconnected hub. As a school leader, the digital principal inspires stakeholders to embrace, follow, and contribute to the vision's substance.

The digital principal, valuing purposeful change, is intent on ensuring that students reach high learning goals, teachers engage in effective instructional practice, and administrators perform well, in part, through the creative and strategic use of digital technologies. This goal demands the involvement of the administrator in all aspects of pertinent strategic plans; it also calls for vigilance in ensuring that these plans align well with the vision.

The digital principal looks beyond the local context to the broader opening up of technology-infused education through policies, programs, and strategic funding. Advocacy at all levels, backed up by research and a sharp awareness of current trends, is required.

As was presented in Chapter 1, the digital principal is a transformational leader, someone who offers a compelling vision that inspires staff to progress towards reaching a common goal. Although the terms *transformational leader* and *visionary leader* are sometimes used synonymously, there is an important difference to note. The transformational leader encourages staff to think in creative and independent ways to find new and sometimes unconventional solutions to problems. That approach is not necessarily true of a strictly visionary leader. As we will see in the next section, the transformational leader works closely with staff to develop a shared vision — no vision is thrust upon members of the community.

Developing a Shared Vision

Your district school board may already have created a strategic plan for technology infusion, but as an educational leader, you still have to inspire and facilitate a shared vision to implement that plan. How will existing resources be allocated and used to maximize student learning? How will teachers be supported in designing effective technology-infused lessons? How will decisions be made regarding the purchase of new technologies? These questions will arise as you consider how to move forward with your technology initiatives.

The journey begins with the development of a shared vision that inspires staff and students alike. The vision may originate with the principal, the administrative team, the principal and the administrative team, or with some aspect of the

The International Society for Technology in Education (ISTE) provides administrators with a standard on embodying visionary leadership. Check out ISTE Standards • A. www.iste.org/standards/standards-for-administrators.

What's Your Profile?

We invite you to fill out the Administrator Technology Profile that appears as an appendix. Taking the time is worthwhile as it will help you to reflect on your own beliefs about technology in education and to identify some priorities in terms of your own professional growth with technology. Completing the profile will help you to focus on how you make decisions on technology acquisition, allocation, and implementation. Further, it will aid you in determining the areas in which you exercise more control and the kinds of decisions made centrally by the school district. Finally, the profile can guide you in the development of your school's technology initiative: it will prompt you to reflect on the processes you have been using.

The inspirational talk "How to Escape Education's Death Valley," filmed April 2013, can be readily found at www.ted.com/talks/ken_robinson_how_to_escape_education_s_death_valley.html.

Former principal and superintendent J. Robinson (no relation to Sir Ken Robinson) recommended this talk on his educational blog, "The 21st Century Principal."

district school board's strategic plan; or, it may come from discussions with staff as a whole. Regardless of how and where it originates, you must be passionate about it in order to infuse enthusiasm and excitement into the endeavor.

One way to inspire your teachers and staff is to show video clips of students and their teachers working with technology in the classroom, or video clips of students talking about being digital-age learners and how important accessing information and technology is to them. There is no shortage of these kinds of resources on YouTube and TeacherTube, and your school may be able to add to them. If someone on your staff is doing something innovative, why not encourage that person to record and put clips online for others to view? Beyond that, you could show a TED Talk by creativity expert Sir Ken Robinson: "How to Escape Education's Death Valley." (TED Talks, posted online, are produced every weekday and always address ideas worth considering.)

Robinson, a critic of standard curriculum and standardized testing, argues that educators should awaken and promote curiosity and personalization. Research into the relationship between creativity and technology suggests that, although using technology may not lead to more creative teaching and learning, it does have the potential to promote exploration, interactivity, and play; it also enables multimodal forms of communication, such as the use of images, color, music, sound, animation, and gesture (Banaji & Burn, 2008; Loveless, 2007).

Robinson reminds us that children should be the focus of what we do as educators, *not* "drop out rates, proficiency rates and growth rates." In his talk, he provides a glimpse of what is possible if we keep our focus on the students' learning and place an emphasis on curiosity and creativity. Robinson points out that any kind of innovation begins with imagination and creative thinking. Imagination allows us to step outside a specific moment to anticipate or think past our experience; creativity is the practical skill of applying imagination and the power to create results in innovation.

Creating a vision for school innovation in technology requires discussion and agreement about (1) school and district priorities; (2) principles, aims, and goals related to student learning; and (3) overall and specific expectations associated with any shift or change in direction of technology use in the school. Eventually, the vision is expressed in a statement that reflects overall goals and directions over a period of time.

A *vision statement* describes what the school wants to achieve over a 5- to 10-year period, and in a succinct but clear sentence or two, it provides inspiration and guidance for members of the community. Sometimes, the vision statement is established by the school district; however, the district may not have a vision statement that specifically addresses technological innovation. If that is the case, the school should develop a pertinent vision statement.

The technology mission statement

Once a vision statement has been established, good practice is for the school to develop a mission statement that aligns with the district mission statement or technology strategic plan (TSP). A *mission statement* is used to define the present purpose of the school, in a sentence or two, but for a shorter time-frame (one to three years) than a vision statement.

To produce a mission statement, isolate the overall objectives in the school district's technology plan, and then, based on your specific school community and culture, determine specific school objectives as they relate to technological innovation. Since every member of the school community should be able to articulate the mission statement when asked, the statement needs to be developed collaboratively and referred to often when decisions are made. It becomes a common ground on which to base future change and innovation.

Here, for consideration, is a sample technology mission statement for an elementary school:

> We believe that using technology effectively for teaching and learning fosters motivation and engagement, and prepares students to navigate the 21st-century world. Our students will be proficient at using technology for specific purposes, critically analyzing online information, and producing a wide variety of digital texts.

Do you consider this technology mission statement effective? Does it include beliefs and affirmations about student learning? Does it identify school priorities? Does it adequately convey the overall and specific objectives and expectations associated with technology use at the school?

In our opinion, the statement offers a good beginning. It suggests that technology use in teaching and learning is important for students in today's digital world, and it identifies what the students will be able to do; however, it should address more specifically *how* students will become more engaged, more critical, and more proficient with technology. The statement focuses on recognizing technology as a connector for community building and the skills identified in it as crucial for students in this increasingly technology-driven world.

To further illustrate the components of strong vision and mission statements related to technology, we are featuring the Peel District School Board's *Vision for 21st Century Teaching and Learning*. The Ontario school board's vision document was released in March 2012.

> Our world is experiencing change at an exponential rate. In order to ensure that our students can thrive and be successful in a future that can't be predicted, education needs to keep pace with these changes.
>
> If we imagine the ideal learning environment — it might be a place where:
> • teachers and students are all learners
> • the focus is more on questions, less on answers
> • understanding is more important than knowing
> • innovation and exploration are part of learning
> • we connect and learn with the world
>
> The Peel District School Board's vision for 21st century teaching and learning is based on the following broad skills:
> • collaborative inquiry to solve real and relevant problems
> • creativity and innovation
> • critical thinking and problem solving
> • communication
>
> Technology, then, is what supports and enables this kind of learning, and engages students by:
> • providing learning — anywhere, anytime
> • supporting teacher innovation and capacity-building

- enhancing equity of access through the use of personal devices and internet resources
- using social media to support inquiry and communication while building social responsibility and digital literacy
- strengthening connections with parents

All of the important ingredients, beginning with the context, are included: the vision, the priorities based on the identified 21st century learning skills, and the objectives. Note that the first paragraph and first bulleted section address the vision of the Board and what an ideal learning environment looks like; the last two bulleted sections answer three key questions: (1) *Who?* Teachers and students; (2) *What?* 21st century learning skills, which align with the ISTE Standards; and (3) *How?* Specific expectations and objectives that will be used to achieve the desired results.

Making the vision grow

Although the vision has likely been established by the school district, you as a school leader will need to work with your community to create a mission statement based on that vision but tailored to your school's context. You need to have everybody on board. Achieving this requires commitment and energy, as not everyone will be equally enthusiastic. Some people will join in immediately; others will need more coaxing, convincing, and support.

It is crucial for the administrative team to create trust by encouraging all stakeholders to take part in the dialogue. Whether the components of a strategic technology plan are mandated or not, teachers need to feel that they are part of the process rather than subject to change and innovation being forced upon them.

At a staff meeting, share the board's technology vision statement, if one is in place. Ask staff to brainstorm answers to these questions: Who is involved? What are our specific goals and objectives? How will we achieve them? As previously noted, answers to these questions may exist in the form of a school district technology plan so your job will be to examine the plan thoroughly and to determine your own school's priorities. In the unlikely event that no technology vision statement exists at the board level, you will have to create your own. Begin by having everyone share their beliefs about technology integration and how it might support teaching and learning. Either way, you will want to have a mission statement that is generated by your specific community, for your specific community.

As a skilled leader, you already know that success with any initiative is possible only when the community takes ownership of it and everyone involved can share and participate. In the initial planning phase, provide as many different forums as possible for parents, teachers, staff, students, and community members to become engaged and provide feedback. You could devote part of a School Council or Parent Advisory Council meeting to introduce the initiative and facilitate a discussion about it; another option is to present a community program night that focuses on technology. You could post information on the school website or Twitter feed, or in the online or print newsletter sent home to parents with their children, inviting feedback. You could also set up a phone mailbox, much like a school mailbox for recording attendance messages from parents, to receive oral feedback, or provide a form for parents to fill out and send back to the school. The form might invite parents to offer feedback on some items addressed in the Administrator Technology Profile. For example, you could ask parents to respond to this statement:

> I am satisfied with the current level of technology integration in instructional activities:
> Strongly disagree; Disagree; Neither agree nor disagree; Agree; Strongly agree

You could then give space for them to explain their answer. Alternatively, the questions could be more open-ended, such as this one:

> Please share any concerns or ideas you have about the use of technology in student programming.

Online PLC Platforms

- *Google+ Hangouts* is a free program that enables online video calls to be enhanced by visuals such as pictures and text.
- *Ning* is an online platform for creating custom social networks that offer invited community only access.

For step-by-step video instructions on how to set up a Google+ Hangout, go to http://www.youtube.com/watch?v=7K06lHu4gDk.

At this stage, the emphasis should be on sharing and developing the vision, ensuring that everyone is in agreement so that they can understand and contribute to the process. Rather than giving responsibility to a small committee, consider creating an online professional learning community (PLC), where people can meet and discuss the issues. Online options include Google+ Hangouts and Ning. These platforms enable groups, small or large, to gather together to discuss a common interest or goal. They can be used for sharing, discussing, and collaborating synchronously (in real time) or asynchronously (whenever it is convenient). Regular meetings can be scheduled, or meetings can be ad hoc; the key thing to remember is that open, respectful, and informed dialogue is critical to success.

Taking Steps to Digital Innovation

In developing a strategic plan, a variety of factors must be considered: these include existing (and future) infrastructure and resources, staff development, financial management, communication to community stakeholders, and assessment and evaluation. Following the six steps associated with implementing a technology-infused strategic plan, as outlined below, can help you address all of these factors.

These steps will take you through the usual three phases of planning, implementing, and evaluating your initiative or project. Within each phase, you will need to identify key people to fulfill leadership roles; establish and maintain communication about the initiative to stakeholders; determine a course of action for the phase based on a reasonable timeline; support committee members, staff, and teachers consistently so as not to lose momentum; and monitor, assess, and make adjustments whenever necessary. How long it will take to complete these steps will depend on where you already are on your technology journey.

1. Establish your vision and goals (or decide on an initiative), and then communicate them.

After you and your staff have decided on some specific goals, you will need to gain support from all the stakeholders, including teachers, students, parents, the district school board, and the local community. In order to do so, you should have a clear idea of the purposes and rationale of your initiative. You will need to communicate your goals and outline your plans in order to avoid roadblocks further into the process. Consider inviting stakeholders into a professional learning community online so that they have access to information and can progress at their convenience. Of course, you are also wise to communicate with stakeholders in regular meetings with superintendents, at School Council meetings, and through notices sent home with students for parents.

2. Determine roles.

Any kind of initiative requires a collaborative team approach so you will need to form a technology committee (and perhaps sub-committees). Members can come from the administrative team, teaching staff, support staff, students, parents, and broader community. It will be necessary to appoint or elect a project leader and to clearly define the roles of the various committee members. Staff or teachers who have advanced technology skills might be asked to organize professional development in this area or help other teachers in implementing the technology in the curriculum. Parent volunteers and community members might help obtain sponsorships from local businesses or organize a fund-raising program. Someone on staff who is good with numbers could chair the budget sub-committee alongside an administrator. Another person, adept at using social media, could take on the role of public relations by guiding and directing how information will be disseminated to the general community.

3. Conduct a needs assessment and school inventory.

Before you formally begin your initiative, have the technology committee conduct an inventory of what technology and infrastructure already exist so that you can determine what you will need to purchase. Consider hardware and software needs:

- What exists? What can be used?
- What is obsolete and should be removed from the school?
- What is the existing infrastructure?
- Where do you need wireless access?
- What areas are priorities if you cannot have ubiquitous access in the building?

Chapter 5 provides more detail on taking an inventory and assessing infrastructure.

It is important to determine what you will need to ensure success of the initiative — expensive pieces of technology are collecting dust in schools because they do not serve the right purposes in the right contexts. Careful planning and attention to the specifications of all technology will ensure that you purchase exactly what is needed.

4. Prepare a budget.

Determine sources (and potential sources) of funding. Consider fund-raising initiatives, district contributions, internal funds, school/community council contributions, government or corporate grants, and partnerships with local businesses. Be sure to separate current amounts available and potential amounts. Prepare your budget with an emphasis on priority purchases. Investigate suppliers if this is not done at the school district level to see whether you can obtain an educational price or a discount for buying in bulk.

5. Develop an action plan, and begin implementation.

An important component of your action plan is creating a manageable and realistic timeline for implementation. If you are beginning with little technology in the school, you will probably want to set up a three- to five-year plan. You will likely not be able to purchase everything you want and need in the first year. Likewise, you cannot realistically expect your staff and yourself to become technology experts overnight. Create a three- to five-year timeline that outlines purchases, staff development, program evaluation dates, and reporting dates. If your school district already has a technology strategic plan and you are working on some initiatives, you may be able to establish a two-year timeline for a new initiative. Either way, you will need to keep stakeholders informed about the progress of the initiative(s) — communicating successes is crucial to your endeavor. Stakeholders will want to know that the initiative is leading to positive outcomes for students.

Sample Two-Year Timeline for the Work of a Technology Committee

September	Determine initiative/project; form technology committee; identify stakeholders.
October	Develop the vision; create the mission statement; determine individual roles; develop project benchmarks and performance indicators.
November	Determine overall and specific goals and expectations for initiative; conduct a school inventory and needs assessment.
December	Do some research: make site visits to schools with similar initiatives; conduct a literature review and disseminate it to all stakeholders for feedback.
January	Analyze needs assessment; consider various options regarding software, hardware, budget, fundraising, staff development plans, and student needs (based on diagnostic assessments).
February	Determine plan of action; create public relations strategies; confirm resources needed; consult with school district officials; confirm leadership roles within the team for implementation phase; revisit calendar and adjust if necessary.
March	Determine implementation strategies; make required purchases.
April–May	Implement staff development strategies; continue to communicate with the school community and all stakeholders; arrange for any infrastructure additions/changes (e.g., installing WIFI, wiring for more electrical outlets).
June–August	Hardware is installed; adaptations to infrastructure are made. Offer professional development to staff and teachers.

September–October	Continue with staff development; begin using the software/hardware; begin administrative monitoring of initiative.
November–December	Communication with stakeholders continues; support for teachers using a variety of strategies is ongoing [see Chapter 3]; administrative monitoring continues.
January–February	Begin information gathering and formal project evaluation (data sources will include administrative notes based on monitoring and feedback from teachers, students, staff, and parents).
March–June	Complete formal evaluation and report; revise plans and implementation strategies based on data gathered during evaluation phase.

Adapted from *Technology Planning: The Educator's Guide* at http://en.wikibooks.org/wiki/Technology_Planning/Timeline. Creative Commons.

6. Evaluate the initiative.

The topic of evaluation is dealt with in more depth in Chapter 5. See "Monitoring Implementation Through Evaluation."

Start with the end in mind. You will need to establish metrics — a method of measuring how well your initiative is succeeding. What performance indicators will you use to evaluate the process? These might take the form of feedback through surveys conducted with students, teachers, and parents, or you might set up focus group discussions with key participants, for example, division leaders, School Council members, and selected students. Once you have collected the data, you will need to analyze it, interpret the results, and share your findings to continue to improve staff performance and student learning. You do not need to be a statistician to analyze and interpret data; you just need to be able to get a sense of whether your initiative is working or not.

Set up the criteria for evaluation of the initiative before you launch it. Over its course, use those criteria to guide you. Review the data to determine both the strengths and weaknesses of the plan, and then alter the plan accordingly, if necessary, to get back on track. This process will be ongoing.

The evaluation criteria for your specific initiative or technology program will need to be tailored to your school's context; however, here are some general criteria to help you begin thinking about your own evaluation checklist:

These matters are discussed further in Chapters 4 and 5, where we address professional learning and systemic improvement.

- Does the technology plan have a mission statement and clearly defined goals?
- Does the technology initiative focus on learner outcomes as a measure of success?
- Have staff and teachers been given adequate opportunities for professional development related directly to the initiative?
- Has the initiative been communicated effectively to all stakeholders?
- Have the appropriate and necessary resources been distributed equitably?
- Have staff, students, and teachers been given adequate technical support throughout the initiative?
- Have data related to the initiative been gathered from all stakeholders, disseminated, and used to inform future implementation?

Working and Advocating for In-depth Learning

For more details, see the full DuFour article "What Is a Professional Learning Community?" http://www.ascd.org/publications/educational-leadership/may04/vol61/num08/What-Is-a-Professional-Learning-Community¢.aspx.

Throughout this book, we recommend establishing — and using — professional learning communities (PLCs) in your school. Basing them on school divisions — primary, junior, and intermediate, for example — works well. Richard DuFour (2004) identifies three "big ideas" that represent the core principles of these communities: (1) ensuring that students learn, (2) creating a culture of collaboration, and (3) focusing on results.

The development of professional learning communities involves administrators and teachers working collaboratively to identify target areas for professional development. A professional learning community focusing on technology integration would feature a group of teachers and school leaders, including the technology lead teacher if you have one dedicated to your school, working together to develop strategies to integrate technology more effectively into the curriculum. Typical PLC sessions are embedded within the school day and are led by instructional facilitators at the district level or organized by teachers within the school. They bring teachers together to discuss and learn about topics identified by them as important, and they involve regular sharing of best practices. We favor a blended approach whereby participants meet both face-to-face and online, as this enables professional dialogue and collaboration to extend beyond the school day and space.

In *21st Century Skills: Rethinking How Students Learn*, education scholar Linda Darling-Hammond (2010) clearly outlines the kinds of practices that administrators should engage in if they are to prepare their students to succeed in a digital age.

"School leaders in the next decades need to engage in three practices that we haven't always seen as part of school administration," she says. "First is constructing time for teachers to work together on the development of curriculum and assessments. Second is designing and implementing comprehensive professional development programs. This includes formation of professional learning communities, providing coaching and mentoring for teachers who have been identified as needing additional assistance, and encouraging peer support teams that address the special needs of struggling students. Third is helping teachers find another profession if they are unable to improve after having received purposeful support" (p. 45).

Administrators need to advocate for their teachers by speaking out against the current factory-model of education and promoting a model that encourages in-depth learning, Darling-Hammond argues. Such learning cannot happen within the existing structure of a typical day at school where learning is compartmentalized into subject periods, nor can teachers find time to plan collaboratively within the existing system — more than a hundred years of using this model has proven that. Darling-Hammond insists that, for real transformation to occur, principals must get creative with scheduling and be vocal about system reform.

You may want to advocate for technology in education more broadly than the bounds of your school. You could take part in committee work beyond the school or school district, and join relevant professional associations. Still, focusing on your school through a technology-rich improvement plan aligned with the school district's strategic plan and through professional learning communities remains important.

Here are some ways to become further involved in professional learning and advocacy for effective use of technology for learning.

Embrace research

For information on the Horizon Project, see http://www.nmc.org/horizon-project.

In order to be an informed advocate, you need to keep abreast of emerging technologies and their projected impact on education. One way to do this is to read the annual *NMC Horizon Report*. The New Media Consortium (an international community of experts in educational tech) and Educause design and run the Horizon Project, a research project created to identify and describe emerging technologies likely to have an impact on learning, teaching, and creative inquiry in education. Each year, the *NMC Horizon Report* identifies six emerging technologies across three adoption horizons over the next one to five years, as well as key trends and challenges expected to continue over the same period. It gives educational leaders and practitioners a valuable guide for strategic technology planning.

Another way to find current information is to subscribe to an RSS news feed or set up a data aggregator, such as ScoopIt!, Pearltrees, or Flipboard. These visual and collaborative curation tools allow you to collect, organize, and share any website related to a topic of your choice. For example, if you are using iPads in your school, you may want to set up a feed with these keywords: *iPads*, *tablets*, *education*, *classroom*. Everything posted on the Internet about iPads in the classroom will show up in your feed, and you can determine what is useful to keep or delete. You can also follow other people to see what they have curated on a specific topic. Doing so enables you to create a current online library of all articles, websites, and resources related to a given subject, which you can then share with your colleagues.

RSS stands for Rich Site Summary or Really Simple Syndication. An RSS feed takes the latest news headlines from different websites and pushes them to your computer for easy access and quick scanning. Instead of having to search for news about how the iPad is being used in education, for example, you can arrange for your preferred aggregator to search on your behalf and deliver the news to a designated window.

Join active and dynamic groups

There is a plethora of special interest groups that meet online to discuss current trends, share ideas, and network. Sign up on LinkedIn, Twitter, or Facebook, and search "Principals and Technology" or "21st Century Leaders." You will find a wide variety of groups to join and follow. These groups will also help direct you to current research and trends in the use of digital technologies in education.

Resources to Explore

To help get you started, we have provided a list of our favorite websites and blogs, as well as a link to a helpful article by Jennifer Demski. The authors of these sites will lead you to many more valuable resources.

Websites

Connected Principals:
http://connectedprincipals.com/archives/5710
Education World:
www.educationworld.com/a_issues/issues/issues423.shtml
Edutopia:
http://www.edutopia.org

e-School News:
http://www.eschoolnews.com
School Administrators' Technology Integration Resource:
http://www.2learn.ca/satirritas/satirmain.html
Tech & Learning: Ideas and Tools for Ed Tech Leaders:
http://www.techlearning.com

Blogs

The 21st Century Principal (J. Robinson's Blog):
http://the21stcenturyprincipal.blogspot.ca
The Innovative Educator (Lisa Nielsen's Blog):
http://theinnovativeeducator.blogspot.ca

Journal article

Demski, J. (2012). 7 habits of highly effective tech-leading principals. *The Journal*. Retrieved from http://thejournal.com/Articles/2012/06/07/7-habits-of-highly-effective-tech-leading-principals.aspx?Page=1

Take a webinar

Many professional associations are now offering webinars for their members. These live online (and sometimes archived) seminars provide opportunities for participants to engage in discussion with other educational leaders and experts on various topics. For example, the National Association of Elementary School Principals (NAESP) in the United States and Tech & Learning offer webinars for school administrators regularly.

Attend conferences

Association for the Advancement of Computing in Education (AACE): http://www.aace.org

Although it is often difficult to get away from the school during the regular term, attending conferences is one of the best ways to stay informed, develop your professional network, and see what other schools are doing with technology. The Association for the Advancement of Computing in Education (AACE) holds three conferences every year for Kindergarten to Grade 12 educators. These include the Society for Information Technology and Teacher Education (SITE) conference, EdMedia World Conference on Educational Media and Technology, and Global Learn: Global Conference on Learning and Technology, which is online. Educators and educational researchers from around the world attend these conferences to share innovative uses of technology for learning.

Give presentations

Why not become known as a tech leader in your school district or even nationally? You can share what you are doing at your school to facilitate the effective use of technology for learning with your school district or at a conference. One way to facilitate this process is to develop a school–university partnership. University researchers are always looking for schools in which to conduct classroom-based research. Approach the Faculty or School of Education at the university in your area, and inquire whether anyone would like to work with you.

Promote sharing of resources

Equity is important so digital devices will need to be shared. Teachers may be able to arrange this on their own, especially if the devices are on a mobile cart; however, you may have to set up a schedule to ensure that each classroom teacher is able to use the technology with students. Achieving this may involve moving equipment around or sharing rooms and moving students around. Having students share a device, perhaps a laptop or an iPad, is often beneficial as they learn by working through a guided inquiry together.

Many school districts are adopting a Bring Your Own Device (BYOD) model, which allows students to bring their personal digital devices to school. However, there is a need to create policies regarding these devices and guidelines on their use, and these should be published in school agendas, in student handbooks, and on school websites. (Policy related to digital devices brought from home is discussed in Chapter 6.)

Below is a short interview with a digital principal who is showing visionary leadership in his efforts to ensure that his school makes effective use of digital technologies.

"Put Technology in Their Hands"

Interview with Kevin Freckelton, Principal, Forest Manor Public School, Toronto

1. How do you build a shared vision for technology integration with your staff?

When we started two years ago, our superintendent at the time had done a bit of work at our Leadership Team meetings by providing data and professional development in the area of integrating technology into our schools. She also created a Family of Schools ICT [information and communications technology] committee — which was open to anyone in the Family (teachers and administrators). The purpose of the committee is to create an open dialogue between innovative individuals and to create a network. Finally, an innovation fund at the Family of Schools level was also created — open to anyone that had innovative ideas.
These processes at the Family of Schools level helped spark our efforts at the school level. An ICT [or technology] committee at the school level was created, and we started to identify areas of need and areas of strength. As well, we started to review the areas of need and strengths of our students based on current ICT research.

2. How do you get all stakeholders on board when it comes to implementing a technology initiative in your school?

A funny thing happened when technology was put in the hands of people that have a background using technology, or at least an openness to using technology . . . other staff members started asking questions and wanted demonstrations of how to use the technology — even the most reluctant adopters. After one year, the demand for technology by staff has outweighed the supply!

3. As an instructional leader, how do you support your teachers in their goals to use technology to enhance student learning?

By providing opportunities to staff — purchasing hardware, creating PD [professional development] in-house, recruiting other staff to act as mentors; by seeking

---

ICT Plan Ideas: Where to Turn To

If you find that district resources are out-of-date, you have an opportunity to take on a leadership role at the board level in shaping future policy. You can also identify a school in your district or a nearby district that you would like to emulate. Speak to the principal of the school and arrange for a tour. Alternatively, turn to leading-edge organizations to gain ideas for school initiatives. For example, the Ontario Public School Boards' Association (OPSBA) has published a useful discussion paper, *What If? Technology in the 21st Century Classroom,* which is available online.

out external opportunities and supports — Apple Canada workshops, UOIT [University of Ontario Institute of Technology] projects, and so on. We've created a learning plan now, based on the grade teams' long-range plans that are required to include technology integration. We will have workshops every month to help staff learn how to use the technology for instructional and assessment purposes, and to build their confidence.

4. What creative ways have you found for funding technology in terms of infra-structure and ongoing as-needed purchases?

This is a huge challenge right now. Aside from dedicating 20 percent of the school budget to hardware acquisition, the school has applied for different grants at the school board and Family of Schools levels. As well, we've also applied for various grants — both private and public, which has netted us approximately $10 000 in two years. Considering we have 22 classrooms requiring IWBs [interactive white boards], we have a long way to go. Still, we're hoping that a new Personal Electronic Device (PED) policy will alleviate the need for the school to purchase a ton of technology for student use, so that we can focus on acquiring ICT hardware for instructional purposes.

5. What tips do you have for other administrators to help them align their strategic plans with digital-age learning?

Start small! Find one or two staff members who are innovative or have an ICT background — or, who are open to new challenges — then put the technology in their hands. It is amazing what happens after — the excitement that builds . . .

3

Learning Culture for a Digital Age

A digital-age learning culture is a learning culture focused on collaboration. From a transformational leadership perspective, the digital principal is called to create, encourage, and sustain a school culture where staff members discuss, observe, critique, and plan together. Indeed, the creation of this collaborative culture is the most important thing the digital principal can do to ensure successful integration of technology for student learning.

The seminal work of Leithwood and Jantzi (1991) confirms this. Having conducted a case study of 12 schools that made significant improvements in a variety of areas, they found that school leaders involved staff members in collaborative goal-setting and created time for joint planning. They also found that a transformational leadership model helped to inspire staff members to engage in new initiatives outside the classroom — they took on leadership roles and demonstrated their commitment to the vision and mission of the school. These new school leaders "actively communicated the school's cultural norms, values, and beliefs in their day-to-day interpersonal contacts; they also shared power and responsibility with others through delegation of power to school improvement 'teams' within the school" (Leithwood, 1992, p. 10).

Although ultimately responsible for your school's learning culture, you can do much as a digital principal to engage others to have a positive impact on it. A large part of your role pertains to providing learners with environments well equipped with technology and resources for learning, all designed to address students' diverse needs. As digital principal, you will strive to ensure that learners gain a relevant education by promoting instructional innovation, modeling effective use of technology, and monitoring how technologies and related practice are infused into the curriculum.

The International Society for Technology in Education (ISTE) provides administrators with a standard on creating a digital-age culture. Check out ISTE Standards • A. www.iste.org/standards/standards-for-administrators.

Ensuring Instructional Innovation

Instructional innovation, as undertaken by the digital principal, can range from ensuring the alignment of curriculum, instruction, assessment, and technology standards to monitoring multiple sources of student data to assess how students are using technology to enhance learning. As we see it, the main focus of a digital principal is continuous improvement of technology-infused learning. In order to transform the curriculum through the integration of sound pedagogy with new technologies to improve learning, the digital principal, as an instructional leader, empowers teachers to enact positive change in the classroom.

Just as we advocate that you refer to ISTE Standards for Administrators for goals and standards to strive towards, we recommend that you encourage your teachers to apply the ISTE Standards for Teachers. These are standards for evaluating the skills and knowledge educators need to teach, work, and learn in a digital age, to ensure that they are using technology effectively. Below, the standards are summarized and expressed in the form of questions:

Is the teacher . . .

- engaging students in exploring real-world issues, using digital resources?
- modeling the construction of collaborative knowledge? (engaging in learning with students in virtual environments or using virtual manipulatives, for example)
- communicating relevant information and ideas effectively and in an engaging manner to students, using a variety of digital media and formats?
- making use of a range of digital tools to further instruction?
- inviting students to manipulate objects and demonstrate concepts and ideas using digital tools?
- gathering student data to inform instruction?

More detail on ISTE's Standards for Teachers can be found on the ISTE website: http://www.iste.org/standards/standards-for-teachers.

As an educational administrator, you need to support your teachers in trying to reach these goals. Doing so means providing teachers and staff with the most current information and professional development opportunities available about educational technologies and their use in classrooms.

Making a shift towards student-centered instruction

As you can appreciate, appropriately skilled teachers are an essential element in the effective use of technology. In the Software & Information Industry Association's *2000 Research Report on the Effectiveness of Technology in Schools*, SIIA authors Sivin-Kachala and Bialo (2000) reached this conclusion: "students of teachers with more than 10 hours of training significantly outperformed students of teachers with 5 or fewer training hours" (p. 10). In general, the convergence of the software design, the grouping of the students while using the technology, the role and preparedness of the teacher to help the students, and the students' level of access to the technology is what influences the effectiveness of technology use. The teacher's job is to ensure that the specific technology (hardware or software) meets the needs of the individual learners and furthers or enhances the instructional goals of the lesson. Be sure to advise teachers that if the technology does *not* enhance learning, they should not use it.

Research on technology for teaching is generally positive and points to several other developments. At the same time that a teacher uses technology, the teacher necessarily adopts a more student-centered approach, moving away from a traditional direct approach. Research conducted over the past decade has found that educator use of technology results in several benefits, such as these:

For a more detailed overview of the research, see O'Hara and Pritchard's (2010) article, "What Is the Impact of Technology on Learning?" It can be found at Education.com: http://www.education.com/reference/article/what-impact-technology-learning/.

- enhanced literacy development
- improved overall student performance
- positive impact on language acquisition
- greater access to information
- increased student productivity
- better student attendance
- increased student motivation
- increased self-esteem

Our recent experiences in studying the effects of teacher use of technology for teaching confirm these positive findings.

The principal's role in all of this is to promote and support the creation of learning environments along these lines. The digital principal facilitates and reinforces the teacher's important work in creating a technology-rich learning environment that invites exploration, collaboration, critical thinking and problem solving, and participation in tasks connected to real-world contexts.

One way to do this is to introduce helpful instructional resources, including websites that focus on curriculum, technology, and innovative digital tools for the classroom. As an example of a resource to share with your teachers, in the appendixes, you will find a detailed outline of a technology-infused unit that is both student centered and inquiry based. The unit outline focuses on cyberbullying (a growing problem in schools and in society as a whole) and seeks to instill in students a sense of civic responsibility.

The cyberbullying unit serves three functions in this book. It offers an example of (1) a unit based on the Universal Design for Learning principles, outlined later in this chapter; (2) a model of how inquiry-based learning can help teachers broach a real-world problem that needs to be addressed in the classroom; and (3) a demonstration of how digital citizenship can be integrated into the curriculum as a way of promoting civic responsibility and engagement. Its inclusion points to the vital role that you can play in fostering an appropriate and dynamic environment, namely, by promoting the creation of similar types of lessons and units that link character education with curricular content.

Modeling and Promoting Effective Use of Technology

There are several ways to model and promote the frequent and effective use of technology for learning and to communicate relevant information to your teachers. You are not required to be a tech expert.

In today's digital world, all school districts have websites, and most school districts host individual school websites on their servers with varying degrees of autonomy. If you have to go through a central management system, you may decide to create a school blog that you can update yourself and have the blog linked to the school's website. If, however, you have some autonomy over your school's website, you will be able to use it to post timely and relevant information on it for your school community. Consider the following options and determine which you will institute:

- Post links to relevant articles or websites on your school website under a Resources tab for parents, teachers, and the extended community to access.
- Create (or have someone create for you) a Twitter feed (that can also be linked to your school's website), and use staff meetings, School Council meetings, and newsletters (online or print versions) to invite your teachers, students, parents, and staff to follow you. You can have your Twitter link embedded in your email signature, printed on your business cards and in the school's newsletter, and posted on the school website to increase your number of followers. You will be able to tweet out reminders about events, words of praise related to student and school successes, and notices of educational resources that influence your thinking or that might be of interest to your school community.

The Potential of Twitter

- To learn more about what to tweet, check out George Couros's blog, "The Principal of Change," at http://georgecouros.ca/blog/archives/1810.
- To see how one school principal provides constant updates to the school community through Twitter, go to http://www.ddsb.ca/school/sinclairss/Pages/default.aspx.

You can set up a Twitter feed in under 10 minutes by following easy instructions: http://www.youtube.com/watch?v=zkWL985S95E.

A sample Teacher Technology Profile appears as an appendix.

- For monthly staff meetings, create a Spotlight on Technology segment. Take 10 or 15 minutes, and arrange for someone who is using a new (free) digital tool in the classroom to present. To identify such a person, informally survey the teaching staff to find out what tools they are using with students, with some degree of success, based on tool types or categories — for example, tools for presentation, research, information curation, and social networking. Working with your technology committee, create a list of teachers willing to share with their colleagues, and devise a schedule so you always have someone lined up in advance to present. For the sharing session, ask the presenter to demonstrate the tool, give an overview of its affordances and constraints, describe how it was used in practice, and share how the students responded. Alternatively, use the data you collect from implementing a Teacher Technology Profile. They will reveal who has expertise where and what challenges individuals face in using technologies to maximize learning.

  One way to organize Spotlights on Technology is to focus on a different category each month, and invite two or three people to participate. Delegating responsibility to teachers who are showing innovation with technology demonstrates a key factor of transformational leadership: *individual consideration*, or encouraging staff to reach goals that help other teachers, students, and the school community as a whole.

  As an example, a teacher might introduce Evernote, an application (or app) that can be used on a tablet or computer by administrators or teachers, or with students. Evernote enables the user to collect and manage all kinds of information. The presenter might demonstrate how to download and use the app, and then suggest how it can be used in the classroom: for example, students who conduct online research or take notes from print sources can use it to sort and organize their notes, and to add website links, complementary images, excerpts of Web-based sources, and more. They can also share portions of these notes with others, including their teacher, for immediate review and feedback. As a Spotlight would indicate, Evernote allows students to include audio recordings with attached written notes. The presenter could say that, in terms of affordances, the app enables peer collaboration; facilitates information organization, evaluation, and curation; and promotes connectivity.

- Seek a partnership with a university, and invite university faculty to work in your school to conduct research on digital technologies and their impact on learning — doing this will provide on-the-job professional development for your teachers. Both authors, for example, regularly work directly with teachers and students for research purposes. The University of Ontario Institute of Technology (UOIT) has a dedicated room in two different schools in the same school district. Teacher candidates, UOIT instructors, and UOIT researchers provide outreach and support to the teachers and students.

- Start a book club focused on educational technologies. Use the professional learning community you have, it is hoped, created to encourage discussion and collaboration. An educational book could be chosen monthly, and interested participants (staff, teachers, and administrators) could discuss the implications of the book's content for their own context and share how to implement the ideas. Budget permitting, a few books could be purchased as part of a professional library for staff, and these could be shared among

See the interview with Principal Kevin Freckelton at the end of Chapter 2.

interested group members. Keep in mind that e-books are more affordable if your staff have personal e-readers. Principal Kevin Freckelton once chose Richardson and Mancabelli's *Personal Learning Networks: Using the Power of Connections to Transform Education*, as a focus book for his school, and teachers discussed how to tap into global learning networks and use them with their students.

The featured resource does not *have* to be a book, however. You could have interested participants view a video, visit a website, or read a specific document you link to on your online professional learning community. If there are more than 12 participants, consider creating smaller discussion groups within the community to keep the volume of responses from overwhelming busy staff members. One way to make a larger book club more manageable is to divide the group by school divisions or subject areas, thereby enabling more focused discussion and collaboration within those areas.

- Encourage and support collaboration among your teachers and support staff to enable the study of technology and its infusion across the curriculum. Doing this may involve modifying the daily schedule.
- Encourage the use of social networking among your teachers to expose them to as many new educational ideas and resources as possible; note, though, that there are concerns to be addressed. Many school districts are developing policies on how best to use social media sites with students and, in Ontario, the Ontario College of Teachers released an advisory on the use of electronic communication and social media for teachers, administrators, and other school personnel.

With stories in the media about teachers being fired for the misuse of social media, it is not surprising that some teachers are reticent to enter the realms of Facebook, Twitter, and other social networking sites; however, you can set their minds at ease by supporting their use of social media for appropriate educational purposes. Share with them the relevant policies in your province, state, or school district. Let your teachers know that you trust their professional judgment, while providing them with appropriate information to help guide their practices. Alternatively, spend 15 to 20 minutes at a staff meeting having your teachers explore the relevant policies and resources. In our opinion, the potential benefits of using social media for professional growth and in your teachers' work with students far outweigh the risks or potential deficits.

Social Networking for New Ideas: Links

Facebook in Education:
https://www.facebook.com/education
Elementary Tech Teachers:
http://elementarytechteachers.ning.com/
Edudemic:
http://www.edudemic.com/twitter-in-education/

We advocate the use of a variety of social media for teachers who want to connect with other educational professionals who are using social media networking in their practice. There are several special interest groups for teachers interested in using social media with their students. The three best that we have come across are described here, and links are provided in the margin. A Facebook Group called "Facebook in Education" provides a venue for educators to discuss how best to use Facebook in their practice. The group Elementary Tech Teachers uses a Ning, a custom online platform, to share ideas about using technology in Kindergarten to Grade 8 classrooms. Edudemic hosts a blog featuring various ways to use social media in the classroom, including "The Ultimate Guide to Using Twitter in Education."

Creating Learner-Centered Environments

In "The Case for 21st-Century Learning," Andreas Schleicher, of the Education Directorate of the Organisation for Economic Co-operation and Development, writes:

"We live in a fast-changing world, and producing more of the same knowledge and skills will not suffice to address the challenges of the future. A generation ago, teachers could expect that what they taught would last their students a lifetime. Today, because of rapid economic and social change, schools have to prepare students for jobs that have not yet been created, technologies that have not yet been invented and problems that we don't yet know will arise."

You can read the whole piece here:
http://www.oecd.org/general/thecasefor21st-centurylearning.htm.

You can read Prensky's article at http://www.educause.edu/ero/article/"engage-me-or-enrage-me"-what-today's-learners-demand.

Much has been written recently about the necessity of using digital technologies to keep students engaged in learning. It is widely accepted that the use of digital technologies goes a long way to motivating students to learn, and we know that motivating students is the first step. Marc Prensky (2005) wrote passionately about the need to incorporate digital technologies such as video games in our classrooms in his now widely disseminated article, "'Engage Me or Enrage Me': What Today's Learners Demand." There, he argues, "if we educators don't start coming up with some damned good curricular gameplay for our students — and soon — they'll all come to school wearing (at least virtually in their minds) the T-shirt I recently saw a kid wearing in New York City: 'It's Not ADD — I'm Just Not Listening!'" (p. 64).

Transition from computer lab to integrated use needed

Lee Jenkins (2012) conducted a survey of 2000 elementary and secondary school teachers, indicating the grade level they teach and the percentage of students who, they believe, love school at their grade level. The results are disheartening. Jenkins reports that 95 percent of Kindergarten students love school, 65 percent of Grade 5 students love school, and only 37 percent of Grade 9 students love school. He argues that students' enthusiasm wanes because they are not intrinsically motivated in school.

We do not claim that technology is the answer to all students' lack of motivation; however, we do argue that focusing on content knowledge does not work so well. Schools are wise to foster collaborative ways of thinking and working that involve critical and innovative approaches to solving problems and making decisions. Students will learn when engaged in inquiry, focused on real-life problem-solving and content that matters to them, and having easy and timely access to information through ubiquitous technology. Motivation increases when students are encouraged to express themselves through multiple means and modes, yet too often schools fail to do this.

The pictures below, taken by one of the authors in 2013, indicate that some schools come short of recognizing the kind of environment conducive to engaged learning. Indeed, as you may know from your own schooling or teaching, the traditional computer-lab format depicted on the left is what most schools still have today. The pictures come from two different schools in Ontario.

Traditional computer lab

Posted sign

Can you imagine being creative or productive in this environment? Why or why not? We believe that students would find it a challenge, something that our research reinforces. We have worked with students using digital technologies to create texts that draw upon multiple modes of expression, through the use of images, sounds, gestures, color, and transitions. Repeatedly, we have found that students' creative expression is linked closely to the connection with their personal devices. When given the option of doing this kind of creative work either outside of class or in a lab, they overwhelmingly choose to use their own devices in the comfort of their own spaces outside school (Hughes, 2009; Hughes & Thompson, 2013; Hughes & Tolley, 2010).

One great challenge we face as educators is how to adapt to the rapid adoption of such personal devices as smartphones, tablets, and netbooks. Market analysts are projecting a rocket-like growth trajectory for mobile computing in general, but for tablets specifically. Yet many school districts still have a computer-lab mindset, where teachers set aside one or two periods each week to get their whole class on the computer at the same time. Even the recent move to purchase mobile laptop or iPad "carts" that can be moved from classroom to classroom reflects this — the only difference with this model is that the lab is on wheels. Instead, we believe, schools should move to an *integration* mindset where teachers use digital devices as learning tools daily to augment the curriculum.

Personal digital devices as vehicles for learning

The ban on (or limited use of) personal digital devices is still prevalent in our schools, and that prompts two questions: How can we minimize the distraction element of the devices while maximizing their educational potential? What needs to happen in order for educators to view these devices as assets to classroom learning?

We suggest that the answer to both questions lies in the ubiquitous use of personal mobile devices and a Bring Your Own Device (BYOD) model. When students have access to their devices 24/7, when they are not trying to sneak a peek under their desks to see their instant messages, when the devices become frequent and invaluable tools for learning, rather than just toys and a means to communicate with friends, they lose their novelty in the classroom *and become another vehicle for learning*. When teachers see students using their mobile devices in responsible ways and realize the power of instant access to information or digital tools when they are needed, we believe, they will begin to value the devices as much as the binders, paper, and writing utensils students bring to class.

When it comes to the BYOD model, the Peel District School Board in Ontario is leading the way in Canada. The board, located west of Toronto, received the C21 Canada's Shifting Minds National Award for distinctive achievement in the field of 21st century learning and innovation. C21 Canada is a national, not-for-profit organization advocating for 21st century models of learning in education. Peel Director of Education Tony Pontes acknowledges that there will be challenges along the way, but technology leaders at the board are working hard to address them. Efforts include working with a vendor to increase equity of access to technology through a low-cost tablet ($55).

As we know, simply putting technology in classrooms does not mean that student achievement will improve. Teachers need to make effective use of the technology with their students. We can fill our classrooms with the best and newest equipment, but if not used appropriately, it will fail to enhance what teachers do.

About a Model BYOD Program

To read more about the BYOD program in Peel, see: http://www.peelschools.org/aboutus/21stCentury/byod/Pages/default.aspx.

To view Tony Pontes, director of education, talking about Peel's BYOD program, watch this YouTube clip: http://www.youtube.com/watch?v=A7zHdGfN530&list=PLUru7M7M3wB9tn66jzRfZcHG0sQGfDRXZ&index=1.

Still, many teachers have moved beyond the tell-and-test model that research has established does not work (Fullan & Quinn, 2012); they create student-centered learning environments, where their students can explore real-world topics through simulations and small-group learning activities. For others, a paradigm shift from a traditional teacher-centered, information delivery model to an active, inquiry-based model still needs to occur.

The need to grow the new vision

As the instructional leader in the school, the digital principal encourages and supports the new vision. In the ideal classroom, technology is ubiquitous and is placed in the hands of the students. Teachers view themselves as facilitators of learning, positioning themselves as learners alongside their students. Assignments, activities, and assessments are negotiated. Peer-to-peer teaching thrives, more real-life problem solving occurs, and students can use their own technological tools for learning.

But the vision will not be held consistently by all teachers, so the digital principal is required to champion it and make it grow. Beyond gaining the skills and knowledge to use digital tools with their students, teachers need to understand what kinds of learning environments encourage student risk-taking and experimentation with technology. In the next section, we review what inquiry-based teaching and learning looks like and suggest how the digital principal can support teachers in creating these kinds of learning opportunities in their classrooms.

Inquiry-Based Learning

The fact that, in the Information Age, students can access information with the touch of a fingertip affects instructional focus. It means that more instructional time can go to higher-order thinking skills, such as applying, analyzing, evaluating, and creating. In contrast to transmission-based teaching, an inquiry-based approach focuses on the *process* of learning to foster deep understanding. Inquiry is based on constructivist learning theories that assume students create or co-create their own understandings through active engagement in the learning process. It is based on the supposition that learning is socially situated and dependent on each individual's background and experiences. It is far removed from the traditional stand-and-deliver model of teaching.

Dimensions and kinds of inquiry-based learning

Galileo Educational Network is a research-based organization that focuses on helping teachers to create inquiry-based projects for their students. According to Galileo.org, there are several essential dimensions of inquiry, these among them:

- *Authentic task or problem:* Students are asked to engage with a real-life problem or perform a task that replicates challenges they might encounter. A task is authentic when students are encouraged to construct their own responses or apply their learning. For example, if a student is learning to create a visual presentation, we observe how well he uses the digital tools at his disposal to construct an effective presentation based on audience, content, and presentation purpose; we do not assess his understanding on a multiple choice quiz or through a written essay.

- *Academic rigor that leads to deep understanding:* We need to ensure that students are sufficiently challenged by having high expectations for them and requiring them to demonstrate content mastery, as well as applied skills and critical thinking about what they are learning.
- *Ongoing assessment to guide student learning and teacher planning:* In our opinion, assessment *for* learning is more important than assessment *of* learning. It is important that students work collaboratively with their teachers to set the assessment criteria. Doing so will ensure that they understand what is expected of them. They also need to be able to self-assess and peer-assess; however, being able to do so requires that they be taught strategies and skills for assessing their own learning and providing constructive feedback to their peers.
- *Real-world connections:* When students make real-world connections, they tend to become more motivated — they see the purpose of the task or project. Connections can be based on students' experiences or interests, or on issues that are relevant to them. The key is to provide them with choice: what is important to one student, perhaps disappearing polar ice caps, may not be as important to another, more interested in, say, animal testing in the cosmetics industry.
- *Sophisticated use of digital technologies:* Digital tools should be used when they provide significant affordances and few-to-no constraints. Ideally, they enable students to think differently, to access or explore a topic more thoroughly and interactively, to express themselves more creatively, or to communicate to a wider and more authentic audience.
- *Active exploration in a lab, studio, or natural environment:* Just as no one can become a good musician simply by reading about instruments and music, students need to work hands-on with the topic they are exploring.
- *Connections with experts in the field:* More than ever before, students have access to people who can serve as teachers outside their classrooms. Simple digital tools such as Skype and FaceTime allow students to talk to authors, scientists, artists, and experts. Many experts have blogs or websites with contact information and are willing to communicate directly with young learners.
- *Expanded communication in terms of wider audience and modes of expression:* Students are no longer creating products for an audience of one, namely, their teacher. With YouTube, Prezi, and social networking tools, they are creating videos and animations, interactive posters, and mashups of all kinds for anyone who gains access, depending on the privacy settings chosen. It is easier than ever to connect with people who share the same interests.

The two most common subcategories of inquiry-based learning are problem-based learning and project-based learning.

1. **Problem-Based Learning:** Problem-based learning, first pioneered in the medical field, is based on the human tendency to wonder "Why?" The intent of problem-based learning is to create authentic situations that foster critical thinking skills and require students to solve a problem or work through a complex case study that does not have one easy resolution. A key component of problem-based

An example of a mashup is a remix of two different songs.

About Project-Based Learning

An overview:
http://www.oercommons.org/community/changing-the-face-of-traditional-education-project-based-learning/view
Research on project-based learning:
http://www.edutopia.org/research-validates-project-based-learning

learning is its inter- and multi-disciplinary nature, which enables — and, indeed, requires — learners with different strengths and orientations to participate.

2. *Project-Based Learning:* Project-based learning is similar to problem-based learning in its emphasis on higher-level thinking skills; however, when involved in project-based learning, students create a product — a project or a presentation that represents their understanding or learning on a subject. While there is a specific, required outcome or product, project-based learning is still focused on engaging students in a real-world, relevant learning process. New technologies make it possible to engage in experiences inside and outside classroom walls; furthermore, they often facilitate the creation of professional-looking projects or presentations. Often, the projects are prepared or presented to an audience that goes beyond the classroom, for example, science fairs or Heritage Fairs.

How the digital principal can promote inquiry-based learning

There are a variety of ways in which the digital principal can encourage, promote, and support teachers' use of inquiry-based learning:

- Ensure that teachers receive professional development about inquiry-based learning, including how to assess/evaluate student process and products. Good teaching practice for inquiry-based learning means tapping into students' prior experiences, linking tasks and activities to multiple disciplines, and making learning relevant and authentic — professional development therefore needs to address this. It will also encompass use of technology. PD opportunities need to focus not only on how to use the digital tools available, but also on *how* and *why* they function within the overall learning environment. In other words, teachers need to be aware of why they are using a specific digital tool with their students.
- Share resources with your teachers through virtual spaces, such as your online professional learning community, or via email.
- Ask teachers what resources they need for their specific projects and then ensure that they have the required materials for inquiry-based learning.
- Communicate with parents about inquiry-based learning in order to pre-empt any concerns or questions they might have about the emphasis on collaborative work or the increased number of projects the students are doing.
- Consider ways to enable teachers to team-teach material as much inquiry-based learning is interdisciplinary.
- Encourage teachers to organize school-based events or to enter their students in district-wide inquiry-based events, such as science fairs and heritage or history fairs.
- Disseminate the results of inquiry-based events by posting photographs on the school's website, announcing results on a Twitter feed, publishing news in the school's online or print newsletter, and inviting parents and community members into the school to view students' work.
- Ensure that the required technologies are available to teachers. Doing this might mean creating a more flexible schedule with longer blocks of time for the computer lab, if that is what is available.

Learning: A Potentially Messy, Noisy Endeavour

Although many benefits are associated with inquiry-based approaches, including deep, relevant, and authentic learning connected to students' prior experiences and linked to multiple disciplines, classroom management issues are sometimes associated with inquiry-based learning, as well. When students are placed in small inquiry groups and are investigating different topics at different paces, learning can appear disorganized and noisy. Teachers have to be adept at monitoring and supporting six to eight groups at once to keep the groups focused on their tasks and activities. They will need time to create a monitoring system to help them keep the classroom organized and the students on task.

As an instructional leader, you need to give your teachers both the freedom to take creative risks in the classroom and the support necessary for them to work around classroom constraints. A creative risk might be the decision to have students use hallway space if the classroom becomes too busy. A classroom constraint would be having students at individual desks rather than tables, which are more conducive to inquiry-based learning. To give support, you could encourage modifications to the learning environment by providing for them in your budget — open table space or benches in the classroom — or by enlisting your parent and local communities to create or donate these resources.

Teachers will also need support with material management so that expensive equipment can be accounted for at the end of every day. Specific mechanisms need to be put into place for the sign-out and secure storage of tablets, for example. All teachers will need to know and follow the same procedures. You could delegate this role to lead teachers, or ask the teacher-librarian, if you have one, to assist with cataloging and equipment management.

Challenges Associated with Inquiry-Based Learning

Despite the many rewards of an inquiry-based approach, there are challenges for teachers and administrators to overcome. Edelson, Gordin, and Pea (1999) identified the five most significant challenges: (1) student motivation, (2) accessibility of investigation techniques, (3) background content knowledge, (4) management of extended activities, and (5) the practical constraints of the learning context. The key to dealing with these challenges lies in the design of the teaching and learning, and in teacher preparation.

For students to be motivated, the topic must be relevant and interesting to them, and if choice is built into the model, they are more likely to be intrinsically motivated. When students have some say in the *what* and *how* of their learning, they are more likely to become excited about the possibilities. For example, in an inquiry-based project we did with Grade 6 students, we found that choice motivated the students and led them to take responsibility for their learning. Their overall topic was current issues facing Indigenous people today. Within that, we allowed them to select an issue (e.g., housing crises, incarceration rates, residential schooling legacy, loss of language) and the way they would represent their learning in a culminating task (perhaps through video documentary, digital poem, music video, or comic strip).

Teachers need to ensure that their students have not only the tools but the scaffolding they need to succeed. Effective teachers are involved *throughout* the inquiry process as minimal guidance during inquiry work can lead to student frustration and failure. When inquiry-based teaching and learning does fail, it tends to be because teachers set up the tasks, provided the students with needed resources, and then set them free to explore independently. While some independence is appropriate in inquiry-based learning, students still require the support of the expert close at hand.

The practical constraints of the learning context can be minimized with careful planning and troubleshooting, and with the support of the administrative team. When working with technology in a lab setting, for example, students are constrained by time limits. Their teacher may have access to the computer lab for only one period of the school day. Longer blocks are much better, and schedules may need to be negotiated. The schedule of the school day itself can be a constraint as students may be on rotary for part of the day.

Wherever possible, strive to minimize these kinds of constraints through collaboration, organization, and resource management. Schools that have wireless access can get around access issues and lab constraints by allowing students to use their own devices for research and preparation of presentations and digital projects. These are all considerations that the school leader needs to think through in order to ensure that the appropriate conditions exist for teachers to use an inquiry-based approach.

Giving teachers practical support

To support your teachers as they begin to incorporate inquiry-based learning, we suggest providing them with resources and classroom examples, such as those found at the Galileo Educational Network website. Videos and sample lessons or units at this site can be used in professional development sessions or in small-team/grade meetings by teachers. The teachers can identify the principles of inquiry-based learning, come to better understand the roles of the student and teacher, and use the resources as models for their own lessons or units. They can work together to analyze what worked and discuss the conditions that would need to be met in their own teaching and learning environments and contexts for this kind of learning to happen. Such activity might also be part of a PLC session, in which teachers explore the possibilities and report back to their professional learning community at the next session.

As a school leader, you can encourage teachers to have a voice in the process. Invite them to list the kinds of supports they would need to facilitate inquiry-based learning and the use of technology in general. Alternatively, do a walk-about, visiting each classroom to observe the students during inquiry-based learning and make your own list. At the top of the next page is an authentic example of a teacher-prepared list.

Check out sample lessons and units for teachers here: http://galileo.org/classroom-examples/.

Kinds of Support a Principal Can Provide: List

Stephanie Thompson was the 2013 recipient of the Reading and Technology Award given by the International Reading Association (IRA). With her permission, we include the following list of ways a principal can support her work in the classroom.

My Administrator can support me by:
- Providing my students with access to hardware such as tablets, laptops and desktop computers in order to increase their opportunities for using technology at the point of learning and to ensure equity
- Organizing release time so that I can gain the necessary hands-on technical experience required to fully integrate technology into my teaching
- Directing school budgets to support the acquisition of new and evolving technologies such as tablets, smartboards, projectors and laptop computers for me to use at the point of instruction
- Improving my classroom's access to online resources that can be used as valuable teaching tools
- Assisting me in finding suitable professional development opportunities in order to build capacity for integrating technology into my teaching
- Working with me and other teaching staff to implement and enforce equitable and purposeful guidelines for the use of student personal devices in school in order to maximize student learning

A sample unit plan that principals can use with teachers during a PD session on inquiry-based learning appears as an appendix.

You can provide ongoing support for the creation of inquiry-based materials: encourage teachers to work in collaborative teams to design them, incorporate inquiry-based lesson design in professional learning communities, and in teacher assessments, establish an expectation that teachers will design inquiry-based lessons.

How to Approach Choice of Digital Tools — Affordances and Constraints

Thanks to digital tools such as tablets, digital cameras, mind mapping software, and social media, students have new and creative ways to explore critical questions about their world. It is not enough, however, for a teacher to say that she wants to use a social media tool, such as Facebook, with students because she knows they use it at home and like it: the teacher needs to justify why she is using it, what purpose(s) it serves, and what value-added it brings to the learning experience.

As a school leader, you can help teachers to think more critically about their choices of digital technologies by encouraging them to explore both the affordances and constraints of different digital tools. As noted in Chapter 2, *affordances* refers to the features or characteristics of a digital tool that make it useful. For example, any tool that enables the student user to add image and sound affords multimodality in terms of consuming or producing a digital text with that tool. By *constraints*, we mean the features or characteristics of the tool that make it difficult or problematic to use. On the one hand, the use of a social networking tool raises the risk of negative exposure to strangers (a constraint), but on the other, it opens windows to the world, which means access to a wider, authentic audience (an affordance).

When it comes to digital technologies, teachers are faced with a huge range of choices. A rapidly increasing number of online tools is becoming available to them and to students today. Teachers need to be more selective than ever to ensure they are using digital tools that enhance student learning. As noted earlier, it is a good idea to set up a forum, whether online or at a face-to-face staff meeting, to highlight effective digital tools to help teachers in the selection process. Teachers need to be able to determine the affordances and constraints of each tool.

Matching Tool to Purpose

The following questions will help you and your teachers determine which tools are best for what purposes. A model review of a tool is provided below.

- How user-friendly is the tool? (What grade levels can the tool be used at?)
- How flexible is this tool? Is it open-ended?
- How do students and staff access the tool? Is it password protected? Does access depend upon students using an email address?
- How does the tool support the development of digital literacies skills? Does it promote creativity, communication, cognition, and knowledge construction?
- Can it be used to publish or share content? If so, with whom?
- Is the tool multimodal? That is, does it allow students to express themselves in multiple ways through images, sounds, gestures, and so on?
- Does the tool allow for accountability and assessment?

A Teacher's Evaluation of Glogster's Affordances and Constraints

Tool: Glogster	Affordances	Constraints
How user-friendly is the tool? (What grade levels can the tool be used at?)	Glogster is quite user-friendly — probably students as young as Grade 4 could use it with the teacher's guidance.	Depending on the speed of the Internet or the volume of site traffic, the program may freeze or refuse to load.
How flexible is this tool? Is it open-ended?	Glogster is fairly flexible as it allows the user to upload images, videos, or audio; search for images, videos, or audio on the Internet; and use images provided by the program. It also allows the user much choice in terms of layout design. The student can choose from detailed or basic pre-made templates, or create a design layout from scratch.	

How do students and staff access the tool? Is it password protected? Does access depend upon students using an email address?	To use Glogster in an educational setting, Glogster EDU is recommended. The teacher sets up an EDU account, and students have individual log-in accounts. Once they have set up their individual accounts, the teacher gives them the Glogster classroom code. This code allows the students access to the Glogster EDU "classroom" set up by the teacher. Having the individual classrooms protected by a password is a key feature, as it allows the students to collaborate and share work online in the privacy of their classroom.	While a Glogster EDU account is a wonderful way for students to share their work, teachers, schools, or districts must pay a yearly fee to use it. That may be a deterrent. Students must have or create email accounts in order to create Glogster accounts. This requirement could create concern for some parents. If a teacher opts to create generic email addresses for the students to use to log in to Glogster, the process could be quite time consuming.
How does the tool support the development of digital literacies skills? Does it promote creativity, communication, cognition, and knowledge construction?	Students can synthesize and consolidate knowledge through multiple modes of expression. They can connect with their teacher and classmates and share their Glogs with a wider audience.	Some students are not comfortable sharing their work in this kind of "public" forum, so accommodations might be necessary.
Can it be used to publish or share content? If so, with whom?	In Glogster EDU, the students can post/share their work in a private space, one major affordance of the EDU account. Otherwise, if using the regular Glogster program, posters may be published privately, so only the student has access, or to the public gallery, accessible by anyone. The Glogs can also be shared on Edmodo, tweeted, or posted to Facebook, which makes sharing through social media easy.	

Is the tool multimodal? That is, does it allow students to express themselves in multiple ways through images, sounds, gestures, and so on?	The tool is multimodal, as it combines images, text, sound, video, color, and layout design to communicate meaning.	
Does the tool allow for accountability and assessment?	The Projects, Portfolios, and Presentations tabs make it easy for teachers to organize student work and assess the work from the website.	Using the EDU version of Glogster does allow for accountability as the students cannot operate anonymously when part of a teacher's Glogster classroom. It is also possible for students to rate Glogs; however, if students are not briefed on how to provide constructive feedback, this activity could be problematic.

Technology can affect what we do, how we think, how we relate and connect to others, and how we see ourselves and others. Digital literacy requires teachers and students to be able to use technology with proficiency, but also to know how to critically evaluate what they use, and how and when they use it. Further, they will need to be able to create or produce their own digital media, not just consume other people's work. There is a plethora of digital tools that teachers can tap into to allow their students to collaborate, communicate and create, critique, connect, and think.

Rather than talking about specific tools, because new tools are emerging every day, we discuss some affordances and constraints of different *types* of tools. Below we introduce five important digital literacy and learning skills to prompt further exploration and discovery; we then offer suggestions as to how you and other school leaders might facilitate an exploration of pertinent types of tools and promote their use in the classroom.

Using digital tools to promote skills

1. ***Collaborating:*** Small-group learning has long been a powerful instructional strategy, and we know that collaboration can play a key role in deep learning for learners of all ages. Using technology to get people collaborating with one another can break down the myth that computers are isolating. While the computer lab model, with its rows of computers sitting back to back in a classroom, perpetuates the myth, the new model of using mobile devices within the home classroom lends itself to fruitful collaborations within the school day; it also allows for students even in the primary grades to connect with one another and their teachers outside school to clarify an assignment or extend a discussion beyond classroom walls. Indeed, we have seen teachers set up a wiki to facilitate out-of-school participation in book clubs for Grade 3 students. Using an inquiry-based model of instruction, students can work on a problem or project by accessing information

online and by using the technology to create a website, a presentation, or a digital story; or even write a collaborative story. They can store their day's work in the Cloud, using such digital tools as Google Docs for written work or a file-share program, such as Dropbox. When they get home, they can each access the files again and work on the project outside school.

The same advantages apply when teachers and administrators use digital tools to collaborate with one another. The tools break down the barriers of space and time and enable people to collaborate at times and in places most convenient for everyone.

There is one caution to make teachers aware of, though. When they use communication and collaboration tools with students, they should be careful to maintain their professional role and not let the informality that sometimes accompanies working in an alternative setting to change the teacher–student relationship.

2. *Communicating:* With the emergence of new digital media, teachers can open up a whole new world of communication capabilities to their students who, until quite recently, were confined to mainly oral and written forms of communication. Rather than writing a standard five-paragraph essay or a report in science, a student can create a visual essay or a hypermedia report that includes links to images, other texts, or videos. Rather than writing a narrative piece, students can use digital storytelling software to tell the story using their own voices and visuals. Students can audio-record the reading of a poem or take photographs for a digital poem using a cellphone or other mobile device. They might summarize their learning about the civil rights movement in an interactive poster, using Glogster. Even graphics applications such as PowerPoint allow students to create organized and professional-looking presentations. Cloud-based programs, such as Prezi and SlideShare, are increasingly popular and offer more sophisticated multimodal forms for creating presentations.

Reading or writing/creating a digital text entails new forms of semiotic processing of the combinations of the visual, audio, textual, gestural, and spatial. Creating a digital text requires the students to consider elements of design as they choose the most appropriate features for effectively communicating their message to an audience. Design choice and multimodal understanding of the communicative ability of how modes work in concert to communicate meaning require producers to be critical readers in making choices.

3. *Critiquing:* In our society of ever-increasing information, it is essential to teach students to be critical consumers and to learn how to assess what is reliable and authentic. For example, students need to develop their skills in critiquing, analyzing, and evaluating the content and the form of websites or video clips on YouTube. In terms of content, they need to examine the objectivity of each site or text, and ask whether it was built on fact, opinion, or bias. An in-depth critique, analysis, and evaluation is essential in helping students develop critical digital literacy skills.

As an instructional leader, you may want to model how to sift through a mass of information on any topic to discern the essential. For example, if your school is using iPads, you could start a Scoop.it! topic called "iPads in elementary education" and curate all of the information that the site suggests as relevant. Invite your teachers to "follow" your topic — you are both modeling use of an innova-

One author, Janette, uses both Scoop.it! and Pinterest to collect articles, blogs, websites, and videos on digital literacies. She invites her students and colleagues to "follow" her on these sites if they also want current information on the topic. Because she has connected these sites to her Twitter and Facebook accounts, anything she scoops or pins is sent directly to her followers there, too. As a result, she has been able to add dozens of people to her professional network.

http://www.scoop.it/t/digital-literacies-hughes

http://pinterest.com/drjmh/digital-literacies/

Technology for Sharing Content of Common Interest

- Although initially used primarily by hobby enthusiasts, *Pinterest* is becoming popular as a way to share events or interests with people in professional communities. Users can browse people's photo collages or "pinboards" and re-pin anything they like to their own pinboards.
- *Scoop.it!* is an aggregator available on computers or as an app on iPhones, iPads, and android tablets. It gathers and suggests online publications for the user based on identified topics of interest. The user decides whether or not to "scoop" or delete the information.

tive digital tool and providing valuable resources and tips on using the iPad with students.

Services such as Scoop.it! and Pinterest can be used for free to curate and distribute content you or your staff are interested in around a specific topic. Not all material that shows up in a feed is useful or accurate, however; the user must take the time to evaluate and critique it by deciding whether to "scoop it" or delete it. The curator is also able to make annotations about the material and whether and how it might be used. In other words, there are opportunities for the digital principal to model critiquing.

Teachers, in turn, can help their students set up an aggregator or RSS (Really Simple Syndication) news feed to enable them to filter, track, and stay abreast of content relevant to them. If a student is working on an independent study unit on global warming, for example, that student might use the aggregator or news-feed collector to gain access to anything recently written or reported on the subject.

4. *Connecting:* There is no denying the popularity of social networking sites such as Twitter, Facebook, and Instagram, and their ability to get and keep people connected with one another. We have to remember that our students were born into a digitally connected world and "being" with friends online is a natural part of their daily experience. What is unnatural for them is to unplug and disconnect from that world every day when they enter the school — connecting is part of their mindset.

Richardson and Mancabelli (2011) confirmed this in in the 2010 Project Tomorrow Survey of 300 000 Kindergarten to Grade 12 students: networked communication tools were the students' number-one choice of tool type. For the 40 000 teachers surveyed, the first choice was collaboration tools; for principals, it was interactive Smart Boards, something that did not even make the student list (pp. 6–7).

Social media networking can be a powerful tool in the teacher's repertoire because it brings together people with common interests. A frequently cited benefit of online learning is the potential to construct knowledge collaboratively. In order for this to take place, teachers must achieve and foster an "affinity space" (Gee, 2004) or "community of practice" (Wenger, 2007). Gee (2004, pp. 9, 73) describes *affinity spaces* as "specially designed spaces (physical and virtual) constructed to resource people [who are] tied together . . . by a shared interest or endeavour." For Wenger, *communities of practice* are groups of people who have a common passion or interest for something they do and interact regularly in order to improve their skills. Social networking sites encourage users to build on one another's ideas and thoughts, which leads to the formation of a collective intelligence.

5. *Thinking:* A wide range of digital technologies are referred to as "thinking tools"; however, we would argue that all tools mentioned above require students to think. Here, we discuss specific kinds of tools that enhance or support *cognitive* thinking.

Graphic organizers are used to communicate learning through visual symbols, signs, and minimal words. They can be used to make associative links between terms, facts, and other evidence related to a specific topic. Mind maps are commonly known as thinking tools, but there are also other graphic organizers, such as concept maps, story maps, advance organizers, and knowledge maps, to help students sort and consolidate their ideas. Some digital tools have been created specifically for this kind of mapping, but other technologies, such as Prezi or SlideShare, can be used to create graphic organizers and products such as info-graphics (the map of the London Underground is a famous example).

Although most people associate spreadsheets with math class, *spreadsheets* are commonly used for making connections between ideas and concepts in a variety of subjects beyond mathematics. Spreadsheets help student develop higher-level conceptual understanding and enhance their problem-solving skills when used to explore questions using real-world data. For example, in a health unit on body image, students can use spreadsheets to compile data about various eating disorders.

Even simple word cloud tools, such as Wordle and Tagxedo, can be considered thinking tools depending on how the teacher employs them. For example, if students are asked to create a word cloud compiled of nouns related to a section of a novel, they are identifying the main points in the story.

Approaches to Giving Teachers Support in Exploring Digital Tools

Here is a summary of ways to support teacher exploration of technologies in order to promote various skills.

- Choose one category of digital tool above, and at each of your staff meetings, arrange to have a Spotlight on Technology presentation. Either you can make it, or you can approach someone else on staff who is proficient with the tool.
- Model the use of tools by category. For each category, select one digital tool and use it with your staff in a concrete way. For example, instead of using PowerPoint at a staff meeting, adopt Prezi or SlideShare, a thinking tool.
- Divide your teaching staff into five groups at a staff meeting, and have each group investigate some of the current tools that facilitate certain skills.
- If you regularly schedule professional learning community time at your school (as recommended), consider devoting one session (or part of a session) to each of the different categories of digital tools. Have teachers identify the best ones to use with a specific lesson or unit. For example, a group of teachers might discuss how best to teach their students how to curate online information. They could examine Scoop.it!, Pearltrees, and Flipboard (similar digital tools that facilitate information curation) and decide which one would best suit their purposes.

The Importance of a Multi-literacies Pedagogical Framework

As an instructional leader, you will want to ensure that, within an inquiry-based model, your teachers use what is called a "multi-literacies pedagogy." A *multi-literacies* approach to teaching focuses not only on students responding to print texts, but also on students understanding how texts are constructed and what meaning is conveyed through multimodal representations. In many digital texts, different modalities — aural, visual, gestural, spatial, and linguistic — come together in one surround in ways that reshape the relationship between printed word and image or printed word and sound (Jewitt, 2006). This change in the materiality of text inevitably affects how we read or receive the text and has important implications for the way we construct or write texts. The materiality of the computer and the Web offers students new ways of expressing themselves.

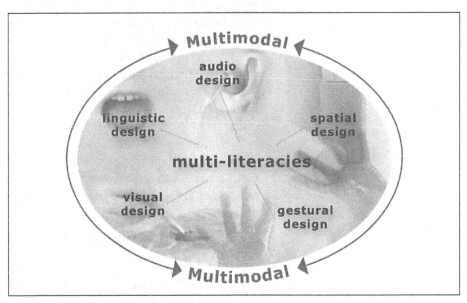

Design aspects of multi-literacies

Adopting a multi-literacies pedagogy will help teachers frame their practice to ensure that students gain enough instructional support, while developing the independence and mastery needed for deep learning.

Pedagogical components of multi-literacies

The multi-literacies pedagogy was developed by a group of 10 scholars primarily from the United Kingdom, the United States, and Australia. Based on a consideration that schools have a role to play in building societies, the New London Group (1996) proposed a pedagogy that encompasses considerations about teaching, learning, and the role of schools in a rapidly changing technological world. The Group suggested that the fundamental purpose of school is to ensure that "students benefit from learning in ways that allow them to participate fully in public, community and economic life" (p. 60).

The Group proposed four underlying pedagogical components: (1) situated practice, (2) overt instruction, (3) critical framing, and (4) transformed practice. These are outlined and illustrated below, using a current example.

Situated practice refers to pedagogy that immerses the learner in real-world practices within a learning community. For example, a school community made a collective decision to create a multi-grade learning garden in their schoolyard. This initiative became an overarching theme for the school and, wherever possible, teachers chose activities and texts that related to the theme. The junior division (Grades 4 to 6) decided to use Paul Fleischman's *Seedfolks*, the story of the creation of a community vegetable garden told through the perspectives of a diverse group of characters. As they read the book, the students drew on their context of working in the garden and made connections based on lived experiences.

Overt instruction consists of teacher interventions that guide and support students in the learning process. In the case of the learning garden, teachers provided students with opportunities to find information they would need to plan, plant, and maintain the garden.

Critical framing helps learners to understand literacies within the context of history, culture, politics, and ideologies. Literacies are connected to the social practices of individuals, socially situated beings with unique backgrounds, experiences, and perspectives. When we use critical framing, we ask students to look beyond a text's literal meaning to note what is present and what is missing, and to think about issues related to fairness, equity, and social justice. In our learning garden example, students examined *Seedfolks* through a critical lens, exploring issues related to discrimination, immigration, and stereotyping.

Transformed practice refers to demonstrated change as learners engage in and reflect on new practices. In other words, although the garden is the culminating event of the school initiative, students learned content and skills in a wide variety of areas, including mathematics, literacy, science, and geography, through a guided interdisciplinary approach. In this approach, multi-literacies offer students a learning experience situated in their knowledge base, accompanied by teacher intervention and instruction to guide new learning critically. As a result, deeper understanding and critical framing of issues or problems emerge on the part of the students. In the final stage of transformation, students change perspectives based on their new experiences and the guided process.

The principal's role: An example

Embedded within these four components is a socio-cultural, socio-constructivist approach to literacy. Our example is based on a school-wide initiative that involves students of all grades in the building. The school's initiative requires the support of the principal in several ways. The first thing she did was to invite interested teachers to take part in a learning garden committee. She also got in contact with the science facilitator at the school district level and enlisted her support. The principal worked with the committee to determine where to put the garden; figure out who to contact and how to get permission from the school district to break ground; prepare a budget for the garden; brainstorm ways of fundraising for the garden supplies; decide whether the garden would be aesthetic or functional; determine curricular connections at each grade level; and make decisions about how the garden produce would be equitably used. Although many of these decisions were left to the committee, principal input was requested at the outset, and the principal was available for feedback as the project progressed.

Support for Differentiation of Instruction with Technology

Student Success — Differentiated Instruction Educator's Package is available at http://www.edugains.ca/resourcesDI/EducatorsPackages/DIEducatorsPackage2010/2010EducatorsGuide.pdf.

According to the Ontario Ministry of Education (2010), differentiated instruction "is effective instruction that is responsive to the learning preferences, interests and readiness of individual learners. Differentiated instruction is best thought of as an organizing structure or framework for thinking about teaching and learning" (p. 2).

Differentiating instruction is essential to increase student motivation and achievement because it means that students are receiving the appropriate level of challenge and support for learning. It also means that teachers must know their students' strengths and weaknesses, their interests, and their learning styles well

Resources on Differentiating Instruction

Hume, K. (2008). *Start where they are: Differentiating for success with the young adolescent*. Toronto, ON: Pearson Education Canada.

Scott, W., & Mann, L. (2000, Winter). Differentiating instruction: Finding manageable ways to meet individual needs. [ASCD] *Curriculum Update*.

Tomlinson, C. (2001). *How to differentiate instruction in mixed-ability classrooms*. Alexandria, VA: ASCD.

"We have a long-term plan to acquire interactive whiteboards for each classroom; currently about half the rooms have one. This is important because digital devices such as interactive whiteboards, document cameras, and classroom data projectors allow teachers to appeal to differing learning styles and interests by presenting new ideas in innovative ways and reviewing information in different formats."

— Principal Jill Foster

Tailoring Instruction

When we put technology in the hands of the students, we are better able to tailor instruction by allowing changes not only to content, but also to the ways they receive or read information and the ways they have available to create and communicate their learning.

in order to direct and guide them in their learning. This, in turn, helps students become more independent learners.

Teachers differentiate by varying the materials and tasks that students work with, by offering varying levels of support and scaffolding, and by establishing appropriate instructional groups according to the needs of individual students. They also consider what elements of the learning environment need to be changed in order to help all students learn. For example, they might ask themselves: Will the students work independently or in a small collaborative group? Students can also be given choice as to *how* they will complete a task — and this is where technology can make differentiated instruction much more effective. Students can choose to express or communicate their learning using multiple modes, such as auditory, visual, spatial, linguistic, and gestural. The multimodal nature of digital media facilitates this process.

As a school leader, you are required to uphold the vision of differentiating instruction with technology, and you can also play an important role in supporting its implementation. Consider the structures that need to be in place to support differentiated instruction; consider, too, any barriers that might exist. Most important, be sure to understand the principles of differentiation and how digital tools might be used to meet the needs of all learners. While the teacher's role is to differentiate instruction in the classroom, the principles that apply to teachers and students are equally true for the digital principal.

The digital principal plays at least three key roles. As a visionary leader, you create structures in the school that are flexible, student centered, supportive of the needs of teachers and students, and based on best practices for using technology to enhance learning. As an instructional leader, you ensure that teachers understand the *how* and *why* of differentiating with technology — part of this means ensuring that teachers have access to appropriate professional development. As manager of the school's systems and structures, you assess the needs of the teachers, staff, parents, and community and respond appropriately.

It is especially critical that the principal be responsive to the needs of the teachers, as they depend on this support to succeed in differentiating with technology. Teachers of all grades will need to set up learning centers in their classrooms with various resources to differentiate for student readiness, interest, and learning styles; you will need to ensure that they have the required materials and resources to accomplish this. While they will require physical resources, such as hardware and software, they will also require time to meet and collaborate with colleagues across content and grades. Your school district may have designated technology facilitators who work with schools, or you may have technology leaders from within your school; in any event, these leaders will need time to team-teach, collaborate with, and mentor teachers. It is up to you to ask your teachers what kinds of support they need and to visit their classrooms to ascertain whether they have the resources required.

Strategic differentiation by grade level

One thing that you, as school leader, will have to determine is how to allocate existing technology to maximize the benefits for the learners in the building. As an example, one principal in Toronto decided to purchase interactive whiteboards for the Grade 1 classrooms, iPads for the Grade 3 classrooms, and Mac notebooks for the Grade 6 classrooms. While any of these tools could be used at any level, his thinking was that students in the early years would benefit more from modeled, guided, and interactive reading and writing on the whiteboard, while older students could use the notebooks for accessing the Internet and in creating digital texts. When considering what to purchase for the Grade 3 classrooms, this principal took into account the abundance of apps for iPads designed for this age group with educational potential, particularly in the areas of reading, writing, and mathematics — the three subjects targeted on standardized tests in his province of Ontario. Although there were certainly other effective ways to allocate resources, he made informed decisions based on current research and the context of his own school. In the future, he intends to add more digital tools (both software and hardware), eventually filling in the gaps in other grades; for now, though, the Grades 3 and 6 teachers are willing to share their resources.

Breaking down barriers to learning

Barriers to learning vary widely. Despite one-size-fits-all curricula, there is not one typical learner, but rather, a wide variety of learners with different strengths and weaknesses. For some students, barriers may be caused by their lack of the prerequisite content knowledge and skills; for others, obstacles may come in the form of a lack of support or advantages. Newcomers to a country face a language barrier that impedes learning, and some students have challenges that are more complex and intensive. Whether a learning challenge is attention deficit disorder, autism, or a visual impairment, its impact on two students can be quite different, even if the diagnosis is the same. Yet students who struggle with traditional pen-and-paper tasks often excel within video- or audio-based learning environments. The more differentiated use of media for instruction serves to reach a wider range of learners.

Inquiry-based learning environments capitalize on new digital media to tailor to individual students' learning needs. These flexible environments enable teachers to modify programs of study and to accommodate their students' needs by providing a good balance between support and challenge. An excellent way to promote and support multimodal, inquiry-based, and differentiated learning is by introducing teachers to the Universal Design for Learning (UDL) framework.

Drawing on the UDL model, new media technology facilitates the convergence of multiple modes in one medium, something that fosters the strengths of diverse learners and promotes greater educational equity. Because digital media are flexible and malleable, they offer possibilities for teachers to design instructional lessons for students who do not have strengths in the verbal-linguistic or logical-mathematical intelligences. For example, a mathematical concept can be taught using visuals and interactivity much more easily through the use of technology than through numbers on a chalkboard (however, manipulatives serve similar functions).

The UDL framework was developed by a small group of researchers who founded the Center for Applied Special Technology (CAST) in 1984. Their vision, which grew into the Universal Design for Learning, was to explore ways of using new technologies to provide better educational experiences to students with disabilities. The framework they created is based on more than 10 years of research in the areas of cognitive science, neuroscience, and neuropsychology. If teachers pay attention to these principles when designing lessons, they will reach *all* learners in their classes.

Universal Design for Learning is a set of principles for curriculum development and instructional design that provide equal opportunities for all students

---

Pathways to Technology Use

Principal Cathy Coon-Brooks explains how her school uses technology to meet the individual and diverse needs of *all* learners:

"Our use of technology has two pathways. One pathway is the access to laptops and specialized technology and programs for students who are identified Special Education students. Special Education students who require the use of technology have access to many programs, training, and follow-up assistance. The second pathway is access to technology such as SMART technology, Elmos [document cameras], interactive hand-held devices, and specialized programs for all students. We regularly explore new ideas, attend technology workshops, and integrate ideas into daily programming. As a team of teachers, we discuss individual student needs and how technology can enhance instruction, program, and our assessment practices."

For more information on the research base of the UDL framework, see:
http://www.udlcenter.org/research/researchevidence/.

An excellent video to begin with is *UDL at a Glance:* http://www.youtube.com/watch ?feature=endscreen&NR=1&v =bDvKnY0g6e4.

to learn. As such, it is valuable for you to make teachers aware of them. If you can find an expert in the UDL framework at your school district or in your area, invite that person to conduct a workshop with your teachers and support staff. If you cannot find someone to conduct an in-service session, then turn to a variety of resources to help your staff use this framework. The Center for Applied Special Technology has created videos that outline the UDL guidelines and principles. You can find these at the CAST website or on YouTube.

The principles of Universal Design for Learning

For your convenience, the three UDL principles are outlined briefly below. We suggest sharing them with teachers at a staff meeting or through a professional learning community. Encourage teachers to adopt the UDL lens.

1. Multiple means of *representation:* This principle addresses the *what* of learning. It deals with the recognition domain of the brain. It recognizes that students gather facts and categorize what they see, hear, and read in different ways; therefore, in order to reach all students, teachers need to present information using a variety of modes, including visuals, graphics, audio, gesture, and words, and through interactive manipulations, such as learning objects or apps on a computer or mobile device. In this way, students receive the information, material, or content via multiple representations of meaning.

2. Multiple means of *expression:* This principle addresses the *how* of learning. It deals with the strategic domain of the brain. It recognizes that, when it comes to planning and performing tasks, students have different strengths and needs; hence, effective teachers will vary the mode of communication expected from their students. Rather than always requiring students to write an essay or report, for example, teachers can provide alternatives that involve a combination of writing, illustrating (by hand or digital), speaking, video production, and dramatic representation. The goal is to have students demonstrate their understanding, which can be done in more ways than with print-based media. Students can learn to create for a particular purpose for a specific audience and to tailor their mode of expression accordingly.

3. Multiple means of *engagement:* This principle addresses the *why* of learning. It deals with the affective domain of the brain. It recognizes that students become engaged, challenged, or excited by different topics and in different ways. Because of the broad range of individual differences and preferences, it is difficult to find a common solution to combat the disengagement or lack of motivation that begins in Grades 7 and 8 and continues throughout high school (Jenkins, 2012). What motivates a student with difficulties in reading will not necessarily motivate a student who struggles with the effects of autism. As always, teachers will need to be flexible in their instructional design, consulting with an identified student's academic advisers and planning with that student's individual needs in mind — something that good teachers have *always* done for every student in the room.

After outlining the three UDL principles, prompt teachers to work with grade partners to revisit a curricular area and view it through the UDL lens. Ask them to develop a lesson that incorporates the three principles and makes effective use of digital media. Have them share their lessons in a roundtable discussion or in a gallery walk (where ideas are posted on chart paper around the room); or, invite teachers to post ideas online for further discussion. A session like this can begin at a staff meeting where people meet face to face and then continue in a virtual space. These kinds of activities provide teachers with the time necessary to collaborate, discuss, share, process, and reflect. To consolidate the concepts, you could arrange for teachers to team-teach or to visit each other's classrooms when they put the UDL lessons into practice.

Assistive technologies

Assistive technologies increase, maintain, or improve the functional capabilities of an individual with special learning needs. Just as the Universal Design for Learning was first conceived to help students with special needs increase or maintain their physical, social, or cognitive ability, though its principles can be applied to every learner, assistive technologies can improve learning opportunities for all students, too.

Assistive technologies offer exciting potential for learning. Specific technologies often include laptops with preloaded programs such as speech recognition software, word prediction applications, and a variety of graphic organizers. Students with hearing difficulties can use software that translates the instructor's voice to text and sign language on a computer screen. Students with visual impairments can use screen-reading technologies and Braille output technologies to access digital resources. Recent pilot projects that focus on using iPads with students on the autism spectrum have found that the touch-screen technology can provide organizational support and improve levels of focus (Herbert, 2010).

Ensuring Effective Technology Practice

In a review of 311 research studies, Sivin-Kachala and Bialo (2000) conclude that technology can improve teaching and learning; however, they note that several conditions must be present in order for the use of technology to have a positive impact on instructional outcomes. Their review of the literature suggests that a school's success in terms of student achievement depends on the software chosen, what the students do with the software and hardware, whether there is enough access to the technology, and how teachers structure and support student learning with technology (p. 7). This assessment coincides with our own observations of schools across Canada, in particular, where administrators and teachers show innovative ways of championing technology within the school itself (Burke, Hughes, Hardware, & Thompson, 2013).

It is important for administrators and teachers to understand and be able to communicate to parents that more than a decade of research supports the view that effective use of technology leads to higher skill achievement in content-area learning, especially in the areas of language arts and writing, mathematics, and science (see, for example, Beetham, McGill, & Littlejohn, 2009; Cradler, McNabb, Freeman, & Burchett, 2002; Hutchison & Reinking, 2011; Sivin-Kachala & Bialo, 2000; and Underwood, 2009). Effective use of technology also promotes higher-order thinking and problem-solving skill development and workforce preparation through the development of technical and learning skills (Cradler et al., 2002). Given that our students are growing up in a digital age, it is not surprising that research shows that technology use in the classroom has positive effects on student motivation and self-concept; however, we reiterate that merely infusing the curriculum and student activities with technology-for-technology's-sake will not result in positive learning experiences for students. Good practice is to see how the use of technology extends learning skills, such as those identified above.

The digital principal encourages teachers to consistently ask themselves why they are using a particular technology. *Why* do they want their students to create a blog? *Why* do they want to have students create a video? The answer cannot simply be "because I want to motivate my students more." Of course, motivation is a key factor in student learning, but teachers need to view technology as a means to an end, rather than as an end in itself, or a learning outcome. Teachers need to be critically aware of which technologies to use in particular contexts for specific purposes; they also need to understand that every digital technology or tool comes with both affordances and constraints (see the discussion on pages 41 to 47).

Why assessment practices need to evolve

Since rapidly changing technologies are shifting the pedagogical landscape, we need to consider corresponding changes to the ways we assess student performance. In *2000 Research Report on the Effectiveness of Technology in Schools*, SIIA authors Sivin-Kachala and Bialo argue that testing the writing of students who are accustomed to keyboarding by having them do cursive writing (for in-class essays or exams, for example) has been shown to result in an underestimation of their writing abilities. If it makes sense that teachers enable their students to express themselves through multiple modes of expression, why are so many assessment practices still tied to pen/pencil-and-paper tasks, such as written tests and exams? Rose, Meyer, Strangman, and Rappolt (2002) argue, "Any test that relies on a single medium inevitably, albeit unintentionally, evaluates talents that may not be relevant to instructional goals — talents that are bound up in the medium or methods being used" (n.p.). In this way, the student is being assessed based on an ability or inability to work with that particular medium and method, something that may confound evaluation of what the student does know and can do. If a teacher is assessing a student's ability to construct and sustain a cogent, coherent argument for an essay, the student can use a variety of media, including audio, images, animation, video, gesture, words, or any combination of these modes of expression.

Rose and colleagues (2002) identify four key ideas to consider when using a UDL model to assess student progress.

First, they note that, when it comes to assessment, a one-size-fits-all approach does not give a fair or accurate indication of a student's knowledge and skills. There is more than one way for students to demonstrate understanding. A written test, for example, is fine for many students but perhaps unsuitable for students who have difficulty processing written text.

Second, they suggest that separating testing from teaching, without allowing students to use the supports to which they have become accustomed to in their learning, does not offer a valid picture of a student's capabilities. For example, students who are accustomed to relying on a laptop for written composition (for checking spelling and grammar, and helping with legibility) are often not allowed to use the laptop in tests because of a fear they could have the answers on it.

Third, new digital tools and media enable teachers to use ongoing assessments that target individual differences in the way that students process information. Teachers can thereby gain a clearer measure of a student's progress or achievement on a specific goal or expectation. For example, one student decodes print text well, but struggles with comprehension strategies such as making connections, predictions, or inferences. Another student is strong in visual literacy and therefore able to "read" images particularly well. A standard pencil-and-paper test would not reveal such differences. By using a wide variety of assessments that take multiple modes of expression into account, teachers can gain a fuller picture of their students' capabilities. We want students to be able to "show what they know" far more than whether they are adept at handling a particular kind of assessment.

Fourth, digital tools that teachers can use with their students include embedded assessments that track the progress of each student and provide feedback to help students improve their performance during the learning process, instead of afterwards.

What needs to be in place for assessing multimodal student work

As noted earlier in this chapter, a UDL approach means that students will express themselves in multimodal ways, including through images, text, sounds, color, graphics, music, and gesture. As this shift occurs, we need to consider how best to assess this kind of work. Wyatt-Smith and Kimber (2009, p. 87) identified three principles that need to be in place for assessing multimodal student work:

1) *"The development of language and metalanguage to shape multimodal assessment needs to be organic, shared and negotiated."*

   When it comes to multimodal assessment practices, the school community, including administrators, teachers, students, and parents, should use the same vocabulary so that everyone knows in advance what is expected of the students. The terms used might be fluid, as new technologies continue to emerge; however, the language needs to be a common one negotiated by and used within the community so that everyone has a similar understanding.

2) *"The development of assessment practices for dynamic multimodal texts should involve dynamic tools."*

   It makes little sense to use a rubric printed on paper to assess a multimodal text. Teachers can "walk the talk" by using digital tools to provide assessment to students. For example, apps can be used to include written comments (via pop-ups) or oral comments within a student-produced video (Mozilla's Popcorn Maker is a good example of this). Teachers can also use the app Good Notes, available on the iPad, to handwrite comments on students' PDFs or PowerPoint slides.

3) *"The assessment of multimodal learning should be concerned with the process of learning — from conception to reflection — not just the final product."*

   Effective assessment is flexible, takes students' learning styles, strengths, and needs into account, occurs regularly over time, and is varied in its approach. Students need ongoing formative assessment in order to gauge how well they are learning and respond appropriately. They benefit from the clear definitions of goals and expectations — students need to know exactly what to do to succeed. Developing the assessment tools in collaboration with the students and providing them with exemplars will help guide them through the learning process.

   We recommend breaking down the creation of multimodal texts into manageable chunks just as you would do when scaffolding a writing task,

The Good Notes App

1. Download the Good Notes app from the app store.
2. Tap the + to add a note.
3. Choose to either create a new notebook or import a document from one of the app options.
4. Tap on the doc to open it.
5. Use the tools on the top menubar to edit your document — add images and shapes, highlight text, and write notes by hand or by using the keyboard.

A special feature, the magnifying glass, allows you to zoom in to certain sections of the text, which enlarges it for easy reading and permits you to write more accurately or neatly.

The Elementary Teachers' Federation of Ontario (ETFO) offers a short
publication on assessment strategies
that your teachers will find practical:
http://www.etfo.ca/Resources/
ForTeachers/Documents/
Assessment%20for%20Learning.pdf.

for example. Students need time to go through various stages of brainstorm-ing, planning, drafting, creating, revising, polishing, and receiving feedback through peer sharing and conferences with the teacher. For example, let's say that students are creating a digital story that incorporates still images and video clips, a musical soundtrack, and voice-over narration. Some might begin by brainstorming ideas for story content; they could use a storyboard or another kind of graphic organizer (a decision we prefer to leave to the stu-dents). Some begin with an idea, then find the images and build a story based on them. Others plan the narrative first and draft the script before turning to the software. We recommend not being prescriptive in the approach: the main thing is that students take the time to plan, draft, and revise based on self, peer, and teacher feedback — the creative process is recursive rather than linear.

Various ways of approaching assessment of multimodal texts

There also needs to be more professional development to engage educators in ways to assess multimodal texts. Jewitt (2003) highlighted that new understand-ing is needed to evaluate texts as "multimodal representations change the enti-ties that are to be examined" (p. 98). Some of these assessment procedures may include distributive assessment, in which teachers and students collaborate on what needs to be assessed; peer-to-peer assessment, which will allow students to help each other with digital literacy; and side shadowing, which lets students assess their work during its development with scaffolding from teachers (McClay & Mackey, 2009). This model provides opportunities for multimodal texts to be better understood; hence, appraised more accurately. It can also be used as a solution for what Eve Bearne (2009) classified as "tensions and difficulties in set-ting up assessment procedures . . . for multimodality" (p. 15), which ultimately affects how teachers carry out their assessment.

School leaders need to ensure that teachers understand and apply these prin-ciples when they are designing lessons, working with their students, and assess-ing student work. Bearne and colleagues (2005) suggest having teachers work collaboratively to establish a common vocabulary to use with one another and their students by describing the features of texts that combine multiple modes (words, images, design on screen), as well as to consider how the spoken word might enhance on-screen presentations. School leaders can provide teachers with opportunities to build on this information as they prepare lessons that focus on the design and production of multimodal texts. When teachers are assessing multimodal texts, principals can encourage a coordinated approach to describ-ing the features of texts that combine image, layout, and writing to represent ideas. As Bearne and colleagues (2005) present it, digital principals can prompt teachers to consider

a) the effect of the piece and the role played in composition by image, design, and words
b) the use of image, design, and words to structure and organize the text
c) the ways layout and typography contribute to the punctuation of the text
d) the choices made about appropriate syntax for the written parts of the text
e) the role played by the spoken, sound, and moving elements in multimodal texts
   (p. 5)

As a way to help move students forward in their development of digital/multimodal texts, Bearne and colleagues (2005) advise that staff, as a whole, discuss what "getting better at multimodal representation" might look like (p. 5). School leaders can facilitate these kinds of discussions during professional development sessions or by ensuring that teachers have common planning time with grade-level partners or peer mentors. There could be a PLC session by grade division, discussion on assessment on a professional development day, or online discussion within a professional learning community. Discussion might focus on some of the following topics:

- How do students make design choices in terms of the balance between the use of image and text; page layout on the screen; and use of color, font style, and transitions?
- How do image, text, sound, and gesture converge to make meaning on screen?
- Beyond the rubric, what kinds of assessment tools might be used to assess students' work with multimodal texts?
- How can we talk with students to better understand their design choices and to provide descriptive feedback to help them improve their work?

Rubrics and checklists have been traditional tools for assessing student work; however, rubrics, which typically focus on the end result or the outcome of learning, are not the most appropriate choice of assessment for multimodal texts. Instead, teachers need to move towards negotiated discussions with students on indicators of quality. These discussions require a shift from summative assessment *of* learning (finished product) to assessment *for* learning (the learning process, which students guide to show how they employed particular strategies and skills to achieve a finished product). The goal of such discussions on the part of the educator is the development of new terms and descriptors during the production stage of multimodal texts.

As instructional leader, the digital principal supports this shift through modeling in interactions with teachers. If new digital tools can be used by teachers to provide students with ongoing formative feedback, the same principle can be applied to the principal's ongoing monitoring of teacher performance. Digital tools of all kinds enable and facilitate collaborative interaction and feedback between you and your staff and between teachers. They also provide opportunities for you and your staff to communicate with and learn from online experts and in online communities. Blogs, wikis, e-portfolios, or other technologies can foster constant reflection and improvement, and can be used by school leaders, teachers, and students alike.

Putting a focus on the processes of learning

New digital technologies can provide greater insights into the processes of learning, as well. These tools can capture the specific learning strategies a student is using (or not using but probably should be using) and what kinds of learning environments are helpful for individual students in terms of their learning styles. For example, in one research study, we worked with Grade 6 students on a social media networking site, where students responded to articles, video clips, and other media they read or viewed online. The students shared these responses with their teacher and peers in an online discussion forum and blogs. We found that students more often combined the reading and writing processes in this medium, whereas when they had to read an article in print and respond, the process tended to be more linear. We also noted that students who were typically quieter in class and tended not to share opinions as openly as others wrote much more and felt more comfortable sharing online. We can extend this principle to adult learners as well and argue for school leaders to use the same digital tools to facilitate collaboration and discussion among staff members.

It is important to understand that part of assessing a final product is to look at a student's engagement in the process of creation. What sets multimodal pedagogical approaches to learning apart from the traditional learning many of us have experienced in school is access to choices of design through the Internet. The student learns how to make choices on such matters as font, music, and images. Sitting down with students and asking them to explain the choices they have made and what they have learned is a way for them to process new knowledge in technology — indeed, this is the new design of learning. Learning with technology can lead to an individuated expertise of practice, which invites the learner to engage in many forms of reflection on learning.

One great challenge you have as a digital principal is keeping up with the emergence of new technologies and determining how best to expose your students to them for educational purposes. Although Amy John is a Grade 6 teacher in Ontario, not a principal, she serves as a good example of someone attuned to new technologies and how to exploit them for educational purposes. Amy noticed that her students were fascinated with Minecraft, an online, Lego-like building game with no specific story. She decided to leverage their attraction to the game by having them use the program to create a fictional, online world for a science-fiction unit. The students found the assignment compelling, and some spent countless hours working on their worlds. The project was so successful that Amy invited parents to the school's resource center and had the students walk them through their creations, explaining the various components of the sci-fi world, including name, geography, industry, climate, and flora and fauna.

We discuss the importance of digital citizenship in Chapter 6.

As a digital principal, you will need to ensure that students are equipped to deal with the ever greater personalization of technologies. One way to do so is through the digital citizenship component of your school's technology focus — more than ever, students need to understand what kinds of digital footprints they are creating. The more we use a specific digital tool, the more the tool knows us. For example, in speech-to-text software, the more a user talks to the program, the better the program understands her. Think about ordering a book from Amazon or purchasing an e-book for an e-reader. The program records the kinds of books you buy and then makes recommendations of similar texts for you in the future. Somewhat similarly, Facebook uses data analytics to determine what products will be advertised on your page. Depending on the kinds of Internet searches you conduct, data analytics will make inferences about the products or services you might purchase. As consumers, we need to know how online advertising works — as a digital principal, you are obligated to ensure that the students in your building learn to be critical consumers, as well.

Although there are drawbacks to using technologies that record information about us, these kinds of technologies will enable us to create learning environments that not only teach but learn. Rather than banning these kinds of tools in our schools (the common approach to date), we need to teach our students to be critical users of technology. Principals can become leaders in this arena by focusing more on students as critical consumers and producers than on "protecting" students from the perils of open technologies. This idea is contested ground, but we urge you as a school leader to be at the forefront of this movement — support and encourage your teachers to tap into these kinds of digital tools and communicate the rationale for this to community stakeholders.

As noted above in the UDL section, new media will help provide students with a wide range of customizations and adaptations as a part of assessments. By providing students with the appropriate supports through digital media, we can help them overcome barriers to their achievement. DuFour and Mattos (2013) argue that, for real school improvement to happen, collaborative teams must be established, and they must use the evidence of student learning to identify which students require more time and support in order to become skilled and which are already skilled so would benefit from enrichment; which teachers succeed in enabling students to do well and so should be emulated, and which struggle to help students and need help themselves; and which skills and concepts none of the teachers were able to teach well, thus pointing to the need for learning outside the group ("Five Steps to Success," #4).

According to DuFour and Mattos (2013), once these things have been identified, the next step is to "create a coordinated intervention plan that ensures that students who struggle receive additional time and support for learning in a way that is timely, directive, diagnostic, precise, and most important, systematic" ("Five Steps to Success," #5). This kind of intervention involves teacher support and professional development in the form of peer mentoring (online or on-site), access to current research in the area as well as relevant materials, and practice. However, as the researchers point out, effective principals also hold their staff accountable if they are not fulfilling their responsibilities to their students.

Read Rick DuFour and Mike Mattos's online article, "How Do Principals Really Improve Schools?" at Educational Leadership: http://www.ascd.org/publications/educational-leadership/apr13/vol70/num07/How-Do-Principals-Really-Improve-Schools¢.aspx.

Promoting and Participating in Learning Communities

Just as getting involved in the local, provincial, national, and even global conversations that educators are having about the effective use of technology for learning is important for school leaders, facilitating the involvement of teachers in these discussions is also important.

Encourage teachers to participate in special interest groups on social media networking sites, such as LinkedIn, Facebook, and Twitter. Each of these sites offers something different. For example, at LinkedIn, teachers can join special interest groups based on specific interests such as "Transformational Teaching with Technology" or the ISTE group that discusses educational technology in general. For convenience, they can "follow" the group so that new posts are directed to their email addresses. Although Facebook is more often used for personal reasons, many teachers and administrators are now using it to establish special interest groups that focus on teaching or leading with technology. For people with less time on their hands, Twitter is a good option because posts are limited to 140 characters, just enough space to share a link about a great article or website.

Although many teachers are already exploring these kinds of sites, some do not have much time to devote to social networking or do not see the benefit of doing so. For those teachers who might not know where to begin, consider building in a social networking component to your monthly staff meetings or make suggestions about which groups to follow. Suggestions on the next page will get you started, but you can also ask your staff to provide recommendations.

Being part of a social networking site means connecting with others and allowing teachers to gain exposure to new and innovative ideas that promote collaboration with colleagues locally and perhaps even globally. If you establish an online professional learning community, you can use that forum to share some well-subscribed teacher technology forums with your staff, some of which are identified below.

Teacher Technology Forums

Here are three recommended forums that you can use as a starting point for your teachers.

- Elementary Tech Teachers is a Ning set up for teachers who want to share ideas about how to use technology in their classes.
  http://elementarytechteachers.ning.com/forum
- The "Teaching with Technology" forum of the Society for Information Technology & Teacher Education focuses on engaging students through 21st century learning.
  http://site.aace.org/conf/k12.htm
- Education Week Teacher provides a variety of forums for Kindergarten to Grade 12 teachers, including one on educational technology. It requires free registration to participate.
  http://www.edweek.org/forums/

You can also use the professional learning community you set up as a communication tool. Tell your teachers about relevant webinars, massive open online courses (MOOCs), discussion forums, and other online communities that will provide them with similar kinds of stimulation to what they would receive by taking part in educational conferences. You can learn about these events and resources if you follow your favorite tech organizations on Twitter or LinkedIn, or subscribe to an e-newsletter via a website such as eSchool News.

If you can budget for it, support your teachers with funding so they can attend a conference. Most large conferences, such as those sponsored by the National Council of Teachers of Mathematics (NCTM), the National Council of Teachers of English (NCTE), and the International Reading Association (IRA), have technology strands. There are also several Tech Forum conferences offered annually across North America.

One effective form of professional development consists of teachers sharing with teachers in-house. Invite your teachers who attend conferences or webinars to share their learning with colleagues. Encourage them to make presentations at school district professional development sessions and at your own staff meetings.

Most important, encourage teachers to talk to one another and support one another in their classrooms. This focus on a collaborative, shared leadership approach will go a long way to improving the overall school culture, and when it comes to implementing a change, should serve to reduce some teachers' feelings of frustration and isolation. Creating and communicating shared values and purposes with a view to establishing and maintaining a collective focus on improved student learning is essential to any school improvement — and the school leader's most important role is creating this kind of collaborative and supportive school culture.

Check the Tech Forum website for the closest conference to your school district: http://www.techlearning.com/events/techforum/index.

Digital Learning Communities:
A Question for and a Comment from Brian Jones

As school leader, how do you promote participation in local, national, and global learning communities that stimulate innovation, creativity, and digital-age collaboration?

As a staff development officer and former principal
By role modeling my collaborative digital community involvement to staff: they see my enthusiasm and appreciation for learning electronically beyond the walls of the school. Staff is encouraged to connect their students to a wider world of learning. Once students are making connections and working collaboratively, staff is more likely to dive into digital collaboration for their own professional growth.

As an instructor of the Principal Qualifications Course in Ontario
I have the honor of teaching the principal qualifications course. One of the many learning goals is for participants to share "technology moments" that allow administrators to work "smarter, not harder." The presentations usually start off with a sharing session of office management tech tools, but through our discussions, presentations morph into participants identifying and sharing various "digital learning communities" that connect administrators with each other. These types of learning communities contribute to confidence building of administrators and a deeper understanding of the role of technology in schools.

4

Excellence in Professional Practice

The International Society for Technology in Education (ISTE) provides administrators with a standard for achieving excellence in professional practice. Check out ISTE Standards • A. www.iste.org/standards/standards-for-administrators.

The digital principal ensures that teachers grow as professionals who implement innovation in support of richer learning with technology for students. Meeting this transformational goal involves motivating teachers and providing them with enough time, resources, and access to gain ease and expertise in working with technology. Communication and collaboration, modeled by the principal, are intrinsic parts of the process. The digital principal facilitates professional learning communities as a way of supporting professional growth. Always up-to-date on the research on technology in education, the principal fosters a dynamic environment for professional learning within the school.

Ensuring Teachers' Ongoing Professional Growth

As you know, teachers in today's classrooms have much to do when it comes to helping their students become creative, collaborative, lifelong learners, able to make good decisions and solve important problems using critical thinking. Turning to subject-specific standards, such as those developed by the National Council of Teachers of English (NCTE) and the National Council of Teachers of Mathematics (NCTM), will help them understand what they are trying to achieve. Standards that have been developed by professional associations are designed to complement the curriculum expectations or benchmarks of a given province, state, or region.

Detail on standards for teachers and for students can be found on the ISTE website: http://www.iste.org/standards.

The International Society for Technology in Education (ISTE) identifies five standards, or performance indicators, applicable to teachers: (1) facilitating and inspiring student learning and creativity; (2) designing and developing digital-age learning experiences and assessments; (3) modeling digital-age work and learning; (4) promoting and modeling digital citizenship and responsibility; and (5) engaging in professional growth and leadership.

Put somewhat differently, effective teachers do the following. They design and implement learning experiences that engage students and enhance learning. They use assessment *for* learning, *of* learning, and *as* learning. They participate in professional development continuously, and they serve as good role models for students, colleagues, and the general community. Their primary goal, as it relates to technology integration, is to develop a digital literacies program that encompasses all of the standards for students: this program will focus on helping students become proficient users, thoughtful critics, and creative producers of digital texts and tools of all kinds. It will embrace computational as well as linguistic knowledge, skills, and understanding.

Ultimately, we want our students to become critical digital users so that the pervasive digital social practices that guide their literate lives allow them to use technology proficiently. As technology is not just a tool, but also a part of a life practice, there is a need for deeper instruction, user competency, and understanding on how technology can enhance a student's lived experiences. Teachers need time to become proficient with technology, ubiquitous access to the digital technologies they use with their students and for their own professional practice, and appropriate and adequate resources to ensure their professional growth. There is much ground to cover.

As for students, they need to have a high level of proficiency with the tools of technology; to be able to collaborate and communicate when solving problems and making decisions; to be able to read and comprehend multimodal texts; to find and use information appropriately; to be able to critique, analyze, and evaluate multimedia texts; and, of course, to be good digital citizens (the subject of Chapter 6).

Meeting these needs is a key role of the digital principal, and doing so can be largely accomplished through professional, or staff, development. Your leadership in the area of teacher professional development is critical in the creation of a positive learning environment for both teachers and students.

Principles for Staff Development

Administrators are wise to make professional development a priority for their teachers. Here, we adapt Tomlinson and Allan's (2000) principles for staff development in relation to differentiated learning to staff development for technology use.

- It is essential that staff development apply to school administrators and other district leaders who will work with teachers. Remember that, as a transformational leader, you stand alongside your teachers so they understand that you are "all in this together" and development is not something being imposed on them from above. Even if you are skilled in the use of some technologies, chances are you will need to rely on the staff development program at the district level in order to provide sessions for your teachers. To underscore your commitment to the endeavor, be sure to attend these sessions with your staff.
- Build staff development on a common vocabulary related to technology use. In Chapter 1, we introduced some terms that are used in educational technology. The term *digital literacies*, for example, is defined in many different ways. The key is to determine what *you* mean by each term and then to communicate that definition to your staff so that there is a common understanding.
- Appreciate what digital knowledge teachers bring. Effective staff development attends to teachers' varying levels of readiness, interest, and preferred learning modes. When it comes to working with digital tools, in particular, your teachers will represent a wide range of knowledge, understanding, and ability. For those who find learning a new digital tool and applying it to their own practice difficult, commitment may be an issue. Some may find it tempting to give up or to argue that they can teach the same content just

fine without technology. Your ongoing support will help them to persevere in the face of any challenges that arise while learning new digital skills.

- Respect that all staff development offers options directly focused on particular needs of particular grade levels and subject areas. A digital tool that works well for Grade 3 students in reading will be less effective as a tool chosen specifically for a mapping activity in Grade 6 geography. Be sure to survey teachers to find out their specific needs before professional development sessions are planned. It would be wise to offer professional development sessions by divisions or along subject lines, with literacy being the focus in one session, numeracy in another, the arts in yet another, and so on. This approach works well within professional learning communities (PLCs). Flexible open-ended digital tools, such as presentation software or social networking sites, can be introduced to teachers of all grade levels, as long as specific suggestions are made about how to use these tools for different purposes. Arrange for teachers to have time to discuss and brainstorm ideas for their own classrooms, working with division partners whenever possible.

- Consistently emphasize high-quality instruction as the starting point for technology integration that enhances student learning. Teachers need to determine how they can select digital tools that will help their students think differently and more deeply, be more imaginative, and communicate and collaborate more effectively. They need to develop discernment — some digital resources offer a lot of flash with little substance. Make helping teachers to identify the characteristics of good digital tools and how they enhance the learning experience a goal of staff development. (See Chapter 3, where we discuss affordances and constraints.)

- Plan to ensure transfer of knowledge, understanding, and skill from staff development initiatives to the classroom. Part of this planning involves asking teachers what their specific needs are and then meeting those needs through instruction as well as follow-up support when they apply new skills in the classroom.

- Ensure that staff development offered in-house is consistent and aligned with technology integration goals at the district level. As an example, one school district in Southern Ontario made it a specific goal in its Instructional Technology Plan for teachers to use technology tools, such as a data projector connected to a computer or a document camera used as an instructional tool, for either whole- or small-group instruction. Since the tools had been provided to the schools for each classroom, each school would then need to provide staff development related to their use.

- Remember that effective staff development that expects teachers to devote much time and energy to an innovation recognizes teacher efforts. There is a steep learning curve for some teachers learning to use new technologies. It requires time, patience, and support, and as noted earlier, if the work is too difficult, some teachers will resist or give up. Your encouragement and acknowledgment of teachers' hard work throughout the process will go a long way in keeping them motivated. Remember to celebrate their successes by offering congratulations, praise, or public acknowledgment of work well done.

Ensuring that these principles are in place involves allocating time, money, and energy to the endeavor.

Notable educational researchers in the area of school improvement have concluded that creating and maintaining a collaborative environment among teachers, and between administrators and teachers, is key in achieving positive school change. Many teachers often contribute their own time and money to ensure that they can collaborate with others both in school and at outside professional development events; however, they cannot be expected to bear the whole cost of what should be a systemic commitment to ongoing professional learning. On a normal teaching day, there is not enough time for teachers to meet, reflect, plan, and be creative — they are already occupied by their regular duties and the various minor crises that arise.

The challenge of time

For more detail on how to facilitate collaboration among teachers, check out "Finding Time for Collaboration," an *Educational Leadership* article by Mary Ann Raywid, published September 1993 (vol. 51, no. 1), pages 30–34. It is available in journal archives on the Association for Supervision and Curriculum Development (ASCD) site.

Schools need to be what Senge (1990) calls "learning organizations," where it is a priority to identify knowledge helpful to the community and to share that knowledge throughout the organization. Finding the time to do this is crucial if teachers are to improve instructional practices and student achievement. Indeed, Fullan and Miles (1992) point out that time emerges as the key issue in every analysis of school change.

You may need to be creative and flexible with timetabling in order to facilitate collaborative planning and sharing time. According to Raywid (1993), administrators can make time for teacher collaboration in ways such as these:

- Schedule teachers for the same daily lunch period and a common preparation period immediately thereafter, thereby creating a longer time for them to collaborate.
- Organize and schedule community service time to facilitate teams of teachers meeting together. Depending on how many teachers are taking part in the work, the community service providers (often older students acting as mentors) can be supervised by one or two teachers.
- If feasible, follow the lead of some schools in adopting a year-round calendar with "inter-sessions" between each term. During these inter-sessions, two- to three-day meetings are scheduled to permit teacher collaboration. Since this decision must be approved at the district level, expect to present a detailed proposal with a rationale for making the change.
- Arrange for late arrival, early dismissal, or elective programs: these can free up blocks of time for teachers to meet. For example, one elementary school in Southern Ontario offers students an elective program on six consecutive Friday afternoons. Students choose to take part in activities not part of the regular curriculum and are supervised by rotating groups of teachers. Every few weeks, teachers thereby gain time to confer.
- As an alternative, create a community service program that involves older students as volunteers on a specific weekday. This arrangement frees up teachers to meet while promoting civic learning and developing civic responsibility in students.

Any of these suggestions is workable depending on how much control you, as an administrator, have over timetabling and scheduling. As Raywid reminds us, the main ways of finding time to collaborate include taking time away from something already scheduled (such as instruction or existing staff development time), adding time to the school calendar, or juggling the ways that staff

What Do Technology Profiles Reveal?

In the appendixes, you will find a detailed Teacher Technology Profile that you can share with your teaching staff to help you determine where professional development is needed. Once you have an idea of where the gaps are, your technology committee will be able to make an authoritative professional development plan related to technology implementation.

Animoto is a Cloud-based video creation service capable of producing video from photos, video clips, and music.

energies are directed. The latter strategy might require administrators to teach or some teachers to assume responsibility for more students than usual while other teachers meet.

Consider providing teachers with release time. Doing so could enable them to meet with each other in grade teams to explore a digital tool they are interested in using or to observe each other teach and then reflect on their learning. For example, teachers may want to use a digital storytelling tool, such as iMovie or Animoto, to have students create book trailers or digital poems. They would need time to learn how to use the technology and then practice in implementing the tool with their students. In many cases, only an hour or two is required, and this would be time well spent, even if you had to put on an instructional hat and take their place in the classroom.

In "Focusing On Strategic In-house Professional Development," beginning on page 72, we discuss some proven forms of professional development for teachers, but before you begin planning for it, be sure to ascertain what kinds of technology training or professional development are relevant and necessary for your specific teachers and the meeting of school goals.

Ways to Foster Adoption of Educational Technology

Although you want to get everyone on board using technology to enhance teaching and learning, your staff will be at various stages of comfort with technology. According to the Diffusion of Innovations Theory (Rogers, 2003), you can predict the rate of adoption of technological innovations among teachers and staff, as follows:

innovators (2.5 percent)
early adopters (13.5 percent)
early majority (34 percent)
late majority (34 percent)
resistors (16 percent)

Most teachers in a school fall into the early majority and late majority categories (68 percent). Individuals in the early majority category adopt an innovation after a varying degree of time, but significantly later than early adopters. Individuals in the late majority category will eventually adopt an innovation, but much later than the average person, the person who typically falls between the early and late majorities.

As an administrator, you need to know in which stage each of your teachers is in terms of the rate of adopting new technology. Most teachers gain knowledge about new innovations at slower paces than the innovations are becoming available. As a result, questions about the readiness of your school community to incorporate these technologies need to be addressed.

Questions to Consider Regarding Adoption of Technologies

- What technology has or has not been formally introduced in the school community?
- Does the staff have operational knowledge of the technology?
- Does this technology have an advantage or disadvantage in its use by staff?
- What policies need to be in place to use this technology safely?

After considering questions of readiness, access, and safety, you can measure the merits of using the new technology in a meaningful way.

Addressing teacher concerns

Challenges that teachers will face in using technology in the classroom vary from lack of support in learning new technologies to a feeling of insecurity about whether technology will work correctly during a lesson. Teachers report that they are overwhelmed with teaching a curriculum already too condensed to teach to all outcomes during a school year. The addition of new technologies still in development as far as their practical application and assessment in school environments go can be perceived with hesitation — they may be too time-consuming to integrate. For staff not comfortable as trailblazers, this is a reasonable position to adopt.

On the other hand, there are teachers who wish to incorporate technology to bring real-world skills into the classroom and to connect better with students already using technology in their everyday lives. Although they face the same challenges as their peers, these teachers may feel more passionate about technology use or be more strongly committed to providing their students with access to digital learning. As they become able to support students in inquiry-based learning using new technology, rather than in rote memorization of a particular set of skills and knowledge, their teaching role changes and with this, the need for flexible thinking arises.

Using technology in the school is a journey that may take many paths and may not turn out as intended. Yet the constant is the need to give teachers support through access to skilled technology support staff and opportunities for staff collaboration, peer-to-peer learning, and professional development.

In order to develop a sound action plan to support teachers in using new technology, consider the following:

- With regard to technology, what barriers do your current staff encounter?
- What hiring procedures or questions address technological proficiency of future staff?
- What professional development can be arranged to address challenges?
- Can changes be made to the school schedule to account for peer collaboration and learning; to share personal knowledge among staff; and to make time for teachers to apply newly acquired skills with technology from professional development?
- How does district-administered professional development conflict with or disregard staff rate of adoption? If gaps have been left by this type of generalization in staff training, how can you address them?

A key way to address staff concerns is by creating a professional learning community where staff members feel comfortable about taking risks and can view "failure" as a learning experience. Risk taking is essential to innovation, but any teacher who implements a new digital tool with students for the first time risks something going wrong. An experience of failure often leads to avoidance; however, if any failure is treated as a positive learning experience, a teacher can learn as much or more from it than from success. Providing teachers with opportunities to take the necessary risks is also important. When taking risks, teachers need to know that there is room for experimentation and that success in this area is not tied to their performance review.

Beyond that, take the sting out of mistakes by talking informally with teachers when something does go wrong with technology, and together figure out how to problem-solve for next time. For example, a common difficulty arises when teachers test a program, app, or device at home and then do not get the same results at school. Encourage teachers to do their test drives in the room where they expect to use the technology — there can be issues with bandwidth or the school district's restrictions on certain programs.

As an example of the latter, the principal had to intervene at the district level so that a class of Grade 6 students we were working with could finish their work. The students were using Prezi to create presentations. After working for a few days and making great progress, they came in and found that the site had been blocked. When the teacher called the school district, she was told that students could no longer use Prezi because there were issues with privacy (students had to enter an email address to access it). The principal then called IT Services and made a special request for students to use Prezi for a few more days.

As the school leader, you can demonstrate and model risk taking, and acknowledge failure. For example, you could use a new presentation tool at a staff meeting for the first time or set up your professional book club on a wiki. Your staff will witness you taking risks and perhaps feel safer doing the same. You can also model failure by sharing stories of what went wrong for you when you were a classroom teacher or in your role as principal.

Rely on your innovators and early adopters to help lead the way. We have found that, once some members of a community begin to experience success with an initiative, excitement builds, and others become interested and inspired to give it a try.

Relying on an innovator

Amy John, an innovative Grade 6 teacher we have worked with, provides an example. Amy decided she wanted to integrate more digital technologies into her teaching practice and into her students' learning. She built a unit on Indigenous issues that integrated social studies and digital literacies, and she designed activities that required students to use a wide variety of digital tools for reading, researching, and communicating their understanding of the topic. Working on some school-provided iPads and with their own digital devices, the students created digital word clouds, digital presentations, and digital brochures. Amy designed and delivered lessons on creating advanced Internet searches and evaluating websites by having them examine two fake sites; they applied these skills to conduct research on the Internet.

As Amy planned the unit and talked to colleagues who were also teaching Grade 6, they all decided to follow her lead, doing so with varying levels of comfort and confidence. The principal was supportive of the project throughout and took time to visit the classes and check with the teachers periodically to see how things were going. The group of five, led by Amy as innovator, was a mix of early adopters and majority adopters, but by the end of the project, they were all satisfied with the students' achievements and with their own growth as digital teachers.

The project created a lot of buzz at the school, and other teachers became interested in the kinds of technologies Amy was using with her students. Near the end of the school year, the principal ordered two mobile laptop carts for the staff to use, and they were booked solid for the month of June. Here, the principal showed an awareness of the heightening interest in digital tools and was able to take advantage of the momentum triggered by the innovator's use of tools.

Evaluating how well teachers make use of technology should be done in teacher evaluations only when teachers have had enough opportunities to practice implementing the technology in the classroom.

Be sure not to push the resistors too hard, though; instead, nudge, encourage, and cajole. Some teachers will not take the leap until they feel comfortable about doing so. Although you can insist that your teachers use digital technologies, creating additional stress will not serve anyone well, least of all the students. Go slow, if necessary, provide support, and keep a dialogue open so that you are constantly aware of how your teachers are coping with the changes.

Stages of adoption and strategies to use with teachers during them

There are five stages associated with adopting educational technology. In their work with the Boulder Valley Internet Project, Sherry and Gibson (2002) identified effective strategies to use in each of the stages that teachers go through as they learn and begin to adopt educational technology. The Project was a district-wide technology training program sponsored by the University of Colorado, the National Science Foundation, and the local school district.

Stage 1 — Teacher as Learner: In this stage, teachers are learning and gathering information, skills, and knowledge that they will need to implement a technology in their teaching.

This is the time for training and practical demonstrations (preferably given by peers who have experience with the technology rather than at an external workshop) and in-service sessions that emphasize how the use of technology aligns with both ISTE Standards for Teachers and for Students and curricular goals. One way to facilitate this would be to provide teachers with the ISTE Standards for Teachers and for Students, which are readily available online, and have them compare these to appropriate curriculum documents for their grade and subject. This review could be conducted in division groups at a staff meeting or during a professional learning community session.

Stage 2 — Teacher as Adopter: In this stage, teachers test-drive the technology in their classrooms, share their experiences with peers, and try to work through any challenges or concerns they have.

It is crucial that teachers have a lot of support (particularly tech support) in this experimentation stage through peer mentors who are more knowledgeable about or skilled with technology than they are. They need strategies to address any technical problems, such as access to online resources, help desks, and open lab times when they can work with someone to troubleshoot an issue. At this time, an instructional technology coach — a tech specialist who can support teachers through the various stages of implementation — is invaluable (see Focusing on Strategic In-house Professional Development, below, for more details).

Stage 3 — Teacher as Co-learner: Once teachers move beyond task management, they are ready to concentrate on finding ways to integrate technology with the curriculum.

The most valuable resources at this stage include peer collaboration, online resources focused on integrating technology and the curriculum, and practical workshops related to content-specific goals. Supportive colleagues within the school or beyond (in an online community) can make a real difference in a teacher's readiness to delve into technology integration.

The use of skilled students as informal technical assistants is also highly recommended at this stage, but it requires that teachers position themselves as learners alongside their students. Some teachers, accustomed to being the expert in the classroom, find this shift difficult to make; however, in our experience working in elementary classrooms, we have found that, even when a teacher introduces a new digital tool, it is the students who discover the tool's special features and share tips for troubleshooting. The function of student technician can be filled either informally by anyone in the class who knows how to use a particular tool or formally by a group, established by the technology committee, to work with teachers and staff at lunch or after school. In our work in schools, we have witnessed students helping their teachers with tasks such as downloading the appropriate program on a laptop, playing a student-created video presentation, and projecting a slide presentation for the class to view. Student technicians can also help teachers learn how to use specific apps on tablets.

Stage 4 — Teacher as Reaffirmer — or Rejecter: Once teachers are using technology with students regularly, they begin to see its impact on students' work (both in terms of process and product). If they observe success in learning outcomes, they reaffirm the use of technology and even share those successes with a wider audience. Digital products, such as videos, digital presentations, student-created websites, and webquests, lend themselves nicely to dissemination on class or school websites, on blogs, and on social media sites. Positive responses from the students, in the form of engagement and motivation as well as quality of output, also reaffirm use of technology and will encourage teachers to use it again.

At this stage, however, some teachers become "rejecters" of instructional technology. Perhaps they do not observe success, feel that they have lost control over the instructional process, or believe that their role as expert in the room is compromised. If a teacher rejects the innovation at this stage, it is difficult, but not impossible, to get that teacher to try again. Some teachers will need more support than others, and the paradigm shift from teacher as sole expert in the room to an expert among many is not easy for some. It comes with experiencing a classroom environment in which teacher and students co-construct knowledge and where the teacher plays the role of facilitator rather than transmitter and arbiter of information.

Here, when a teacher has rejected innovation, the support of the administrator is most crucial. Ways to directly transform your "rejecters" into "adopters" include partnering them with a peer mentor who is enthusiastic about technology integration, providing them with release time to gain further professional development, arranging for an instructional technology coach to work directly with them, and, in some cases, taking the pressure off by slowing down the process of adoption.

Note, though, that teachers can feel pressure to use more and more technology even when you as digital principal are not putting it on. Pressure can come from students, parents, colleagues, and from within — teachers understand that they live in a digital age and need to "keep up with the times." Letting your teachers know that they can take just baby steps as long as they are moving forward will do much to reduce the pressure they might be under.

Stage 5 — Teacher as Leader: With greater experience, teachers become more knowledgeable, skilled, and comfortable using technology. They begin to share their experiences with other teachers, taking on the role of mentor or leader. They may even lead workshops for other staff and become pivotal members of your in-house professional development program. You can support these teacher-leaders

Adoption Stages: Summary

1. Teacher as Learner
2. Teacher as Adopter
3. Teacher as Co-learner
4. Teacher as Reaffirmer (or Rejecter)
5. Teacher as Leader

by providing them with the necessary resources, such as release time to coach or co-teach with others. In terms of bottom-up change, the technology leaders, or innovators, are your most valuable asset — be sure to offer them the acknowledgment and recognition they deserve.

Focusing On Strategic In-house Professional Development

Many school districts offer a variety of PD sessions related to their technology-strategic plans, and they target specific grades and subject areas. For example, one school district offers a session for Kindergarten to Grade 3 teachers that focuses on the use of presentation tools and online resources. It also offers a session for Grades 4 to 6 teachers that focuses on using multimedia tools such as comic-strip generators, as well as website creation and digital storytelling software for social studies. Encourage teaching staff to take part in such learning opportunities, but be aware of the limitations of this kind of approach.

Districts may require teachers to complete a course or a series of workshops before they are equipped with an interactive whiteboard for their classroom or allocated a set of classroom iPads. The problem with this approach, in which organizers decide what's important, is that a one-size-fits-all training program cannot meet the needs of individual teachers. What is better is for you and your teachers to develop an in-house model of professional development. In-house models more effectively target the individual needs of teachers and the school within their specific contexts. Yet, as in the district programs, you may be able to encourage participation and engagement by making the technology the incentive.

Effective professional development in technology is job embedded and ongoing, and it focuses on both the subject material and the digital tools that the teacher is teaching or using (or planning to use) with the students. Decisions about it involve the teachers and relate, not only to their individual needs, but also to the specific context and the goals of the school community.

Inviting teachers to give feedback or evaluate their professional development is a good idea so you can improve your approach moving forward. As you begin to plan in-house PD opportunities for your staff, consider creating a multi-faceted program that combines the use of demonstrations, hands-on activities, and time for questions and answers; include print or online video instructions for using the digital tool so that teachers can extend their knowledge after the session ends.

A typical 60-minute session geared towards the introduction of a new iPad app might look like this:

- Overview of the Digital Tool (participants download the app): 5 minutes
- Demonstration of the Digital Tool with Print and Video Support (with participants following along on the app): 10–15 minutes
- Hands-on Exploration of the App (playing with features, creating an example): 20–30 minutes
- Discussion/Collaboration Time (participants explore curricular applications for the app): 10–15 minutes
- Online or Real-Time Follow-up (participants share how they use the app with students): unlimited time

Another session might focus on technology at the point of learning. Further to that, you will find, as an appendix, a sample unit plan that integrates technology using an inquiry-based approach. You could have your teachers look over the plan, discuss its features, and perhaps use it as a model to create a lesson plan or unit they could use with their own students.

A good idea is to provide time and space for teachers to reflect on their learning. They can do this immediately after the session, of course, but encourage it over time, as well. Teachers will want to share their experiences actually using the digital tools with their students. An online space, such as a Google+ Hangout or a wiki, would allow them to discuss challenges and successes at their own convenience, or they could share ideas during their team planning meetings. You could post a question in your online professional learning community space to prompt teachers to share. Alternatively, you could set up (or have someone set up for you) a Celly group specifically for session attendees. *Celly* is an iPhone and iPad app that allows invited members of a group to instant-message each other; communication is thereby immediate and members of the group are constantly connected. These conditions invite collaborative problem-solving and critical thinking as a collective.

Celly was used by the Occupy Wall Street's Tech Ops Working Group to provide instant updates to more than 5000 people in the Occupy Wall Street movement. For more information on the app, go to http://cel.ly.

Ideas for in-house professional development

Consider the following in-house PD ideas whose implementation has proven effective for a variety of schools across North America.

Targeted Professional Development: After you have done a needs assessment based on Teacher Technology Profile results, encourage your teachers to develop their own professional growth plans for technology. In Alberta, for example, all teachers are required to develop a professional growth plan that includes specific goals, strategies to meet those goals, a timeline, indicators or measures of success, and reflections on their professional growth in terms of implications for future practice.

Professional Growth Plan

Every administrator and teacher is wise to create a professional growth plan. In your plan, be sure to identify where you need to grow and which areas should be priorities based on the school's technology initiatives and plans.

There are different approaches to developing a growth plan. A number of templates, including graphic organizers and various ways to frame the plan, are available online to help teachers. One simple set of criteria can be developed using the *what and how* model: What will I achieve? How will I achieve it? What resources do I have? What do I need to have in order to achieve my goals? How will I know if I have succeeded in achieving my goals? What data or information can I collect to help me reflect on my success in achieving my goals? How will I change my practice as a result of my experiences?

For more guidance, criteria, and templates on creating professional growth plans, see the Alberta Teachers' Association website: www.teachers.ab.ca.

Once teachers have identified the areas in which they need to grow, invite individuals to submit a proposal to attend a PD session that targets an area of need. Circulate to your staff a list of PD events to consider. Post in the office or online on your PLC platform a record of the sessions your teachers have attended so that the whole community can know who is now knowledgeable in specific areas. Be sure to schedule subsequent workshops or sharing sessions for the whole staff using the Teach the Teachers model (below). Even though teachers may attend some external PD sessions, having them share their learning with colleagues ensures that everyone in the building benefits.

Teach the Teachers: Whenever one of your teachers attends a conference or workshop, make it an expectation that the teacher will share the new material,

Resource on Instructional Rounds

Marzano, R. J. (2011, February). The art & science of teaching: Making the most of instructional rounds. *Instructional Leadership, 60*(5), 80–82. http://www.ascd.org/publications/educational-leadership/feb11/vol68/num05/Making-the-Most-of-Instructional-Rounds.aspx

Recommended Book Club Titles

- *The Anti-Education Era: Creating Smarter Students Through Digital Learning* by James Paul Gee (2013) Gee's talk about his book on YouTube:
  http://www.youtube.com/watch?v=ryAt38IJjH8
- *Personal Learning Networks: Using the Power of Connections to Transform Education* by Will Richardson and Rob Mancabelli (2011) Richardson's wiki on creating personal learning networks:
  https://weblogged.wikispaces.com/Personal+Learning+Networks His explanation of personal learning networks on YouTube:
  http://www.youtube.com/watch?v=mghGV37TeK8

resources, and learning with the rest of the staff upon returning. This sharing can be done at a staff meeting or on a professional development half-day when there are several people who have received external training or professional development. These sessions can also be set up as "brown-bag" or potluck lunches so that teachers can make productive use of the lunch break. In this model, both presenters and attendees benefit: presenters can consolidate their learning by sharing it with others and thereby take on a leadership role within the school; attendees learn about a new concept or digital tool for teaching and learning. As principal, you benefit by maximizing the use of your PD funds while building leadership capacity within the school.

Instructional Rounds: Probably all of us have attended a professional development session in which we listened to someone share great ideas about an innovative teaching strategy or assessment tool; however, we may also have had the experience that, until we see the strategy or tool in action or try to put it into practice, there is no change in or impact on what we do.

An "instructional rounds" approach, based on the medical practice of interns learning from experienced doctors, offers teachers the opportunity to see a lesson/activity or digital technology in use in the classroom context. It provides an authentic experience in that observers see how something works in the world of the classroom. A lead teacher (with co-teachers or alone) plans a lesson using a digital tool or tools, and a group of teachers sit in on the lesson to observe. After the lesson, with everything still fresh in their minds, the whole group meets outside the classroom to discuss and reflect on what happened. This debriefing is not meant to be evaluative. The lead teacher is expected to remind participants that the intention is to discuss the strengths and challenges of using the digital technology chosen, as well as the students' responses and any new ideas for using the same technology in another way (Marzano, 2011).

Virtual Book Clubs: Work with the technology team or committee you have established (see Chapter 2) to select a Principal's Book of the Month, maybe a picture book, a professional book, or a novel. Be sure to select digital texts, such as a video or an online article, occasionally or to supplement the reading of a print book or e-book with related YouTube clips. Principal Kevin Freckelton, for example, has chosen Will Richardson's e-book, *Why School? How Education Must Change When Learning and Information Are Everywhere*, published by TED Books in 2012, as a focus. Kevin notes that they do not "have everyone on the bus (yet)," but the e-book and corresponding TED talk (at https://www.youtube.com/watch?v=9ekcWQxgk3k) provided a good springboard for conversations, particularly among those using a 21st century lens.

For your book club, set up a virtual space for interested teachers to discuss the book; as appropriate, the teachers can also create and share related lesson plans that use digital technologies. You can lead the discussion yourself or arrange for a technology team member (or other volunteer) to do it. In any event, be sure to take part so that your staff sees that you are committed to the endeavor.

School Site Visits and School Partnerships: At your regular school district principals' meetings or at administrator conferences, ask your colleagues what kinds of technology initiatives they are undertaking. If another school in your area is doing something innovative with technology, send a small team of your teachers for a site visit to observe best practices. Set up an ongoing partnership with a nearby school, and teach and support each other based on your respective strengths.

Technology Coaching: Where to Look

To find out more about instructional technology coaching:
http://educationismylife.com/instructional-technology-professional-development-by-design/

To learn more about the ISTE Standards for Coaches:
http://www.iste.org/docs/pdfs/nets-c.pdf?sfvrsn=2

Coaching: Traditional approaches to professional development in technology often involve teaching a specific digital tool and perhaps the best practices associated with using the tool at a certain grade level; however, it is also important to offer continual support, and coaching is one way to do this.

Many school districts in North America have designated coaches, called "instructional technology coaches" in the United States and "educational technology facilitators" in Canada. The International Society for Technology in Education even has a set of standards for coaches. A coach supports and guides teachers through the various stages of technology implementation, including planning. Before the lesson or unit is taught, the coach helps the teacher to plan content-specific learning activities based on curricular goals. During the lesson(s) involving technology, the coach is in the classroom, providing instructional and technological support, often team-teaching with the classroom teacher. After the lesson, the teacher and coach meet to reflect on the successes and challenges experienced. The coach ensures that the teacher will be comfortable implementing the technology in future lessons. This context-specific approach makes professional development relevant, applicable, and purposeful.

Mentorship Programs: Most, if not all, school districts now have new teacher induction or mentoring programs. Some of these are informal arrangements, but many are now required and are formal in their execution. However, mentoring is not only beneficial to new teachers; it is also helpful for more experienced teachers to have in-service and mentoring in the effective use of technology. In fact, some of the newest teachers are most proficient with new technologies.

The principal's role in establishing and monitoring the mentoring process is crucial. Here is what to do:

- Meet with teachers new to the school when they are hired to discuss their strengths and areas of need related to technology.
- Facilitate an appropriate partnership when matching mentors with teachers new to the school or current teachers who would benefit from tech mentorship.
- Facilitate joint growth planning for both participants.
- Ensure that both participants have the supports they need to make the partnership successful: these include allocating sufficient funding, time, and resources.
- Monitor the progress of the mentoring program and meet with the individuals on a regular schedule.
- Help both participants in making any tweaks to the program or plans as needed.

Opening Up Communication Among Stakeholders

Effective school leaders know that communication is an essential leadership skill and apply the skill. How are you currently communicating with the stakeholders in your community? Is the communication one-way or two-way? How do you promote communication among stakeholders? The traditional print newsletter that is sent home to parents is a way to share news, update parents on the progress of initiatives, and celebrate the school's successes, but it has limitations. For starters, communication flows only in one direction — from the school to the home. In order to respond to something in the newsletter, a parent has to call or write a note to the school. To facilitate a dialogue, you could go online and communicate through your school blog or website, or by using social media and invite comments from your readers. This model opens up the conversation for anyone to participate. You would thereby be environmentally conscious while reducing school expenditures.

Some schools send home the September newsletter in print form with a notification that subsequent newsletters will be available only online at the school's website. If a paper copy is required because a family does not have access to the Internet or if they just prefer to read a print copy, the family notifies the school and a paper copy continues to be sent home monthly. To avoid any stigma being attached to the choice, parents do not have to disclose why they prefer a print copy. An online or print newsletter sends families all of the school news at once with dates for upcoming events. Families can then transfer these dates to their calendars so they don't miss them.

A Twitter feed would allow you (or someone in your office) to issue communications, announcements, and reminders to your stakeholders as the need arises. You would not have to wait until the next month to celebrate the success of a sports team or to announce a student award. In addition, your Twitter followers could reply to any post you send, opening up conversation for anyone to join.

Blogs for Comment on Issues

Consider using a blog that either links to your school's website or houses it. Most school websites sit on the school district's server, which means that to make any changes to the site, the person who maintains it must have the necessary training or expertise, or needs to put in a request to a central communications department to make the change on the school's behalf. This cumbersome process makes it less likely that updates will be made frequently. If your school district allows you to create and maintain your own website, a blogging engine may offer you more flexibility in terms of customization. Most blog engines allow those who are following the blog to post comments in response, so conversation among many stakeholders is possible.

Many of your communication needs can be met with a blog that enables you to share news with staff, parents, and the broader community on a regular basis. If you do decide on a blog, you will need to commit to blogging often and at regular intervals. If you have a lot to say and like sharing your views on educational issues, blogging may suit your purposes better than Twitter, which limits tweets to 140 characters each. Both Twitter and blogs allow you to model the effective use of social media, while promoting your school; however, principals who blog typically comment on articles or books they have read, conferences they have attended, and trends or policies that are current; they also embed photos and videos in their blogs. Rather than making announcements about school events, blogs tend to be used for commenting on issues and raising questions for discussion.

Model Twitter Feed

Eric Sheninger is an award-winning digital principal. You can see his Twitter feed here: https://twitter.com/NMHS_Principal.

Inspiring Blogs to Follow

When it comes to writing blogs, a number of principals are leading the way. If you want initial inspiration, here are a few excellent blogs to follow.

- George Couros's award-winning blog, "The Principal of Change: Stories of Learning and Leading," focuses on leading innovation and change. Couros is interested in the use of social media for administrators and shares his experiences as a digital principal, educational speaker, and workshop leader. http://georgecouros.ca/blog/
- Award-winning principal Mike King's blog, "The Digital Sandbox," focuses on all aspects of digital learning, from the art of digital storytelling to the flipped classroom, where educators prepare videos for students to use outside class so that class time for hands-on exploration and interaction can be maximized. http://digitalsandbox.weebly.com/
- Patrick Larkin is a former principal turned assistant superintendent for learning. His daily blog focuses on school reform and technology integration. For October 2013 (Connected Educator Month), Larkin used his blog to highlight the profiles of American educators who are using technology effectively. www.patrickmlarkin.com

Obviously, face-to-face communication, as well as email and telephone, is desirable in certain situations. Indeed, face-to-face meetings involving students, parents/guardians, teachers, and administrators are essential when dealing with matters that require sensitivity, privacy, transparency, and relationship building. Email and telephone are appropriate and convenient tools for many aspects of work, including scheduling meetings, asking peers and colleagues quick questions, or communicating with school district personnel about various matters. Your communication toolkit may include conference calls, email, texts, video conferences, and social media networks; however, none of these tools can convey tone, gesture, facial expression, and body language as well as a face-to-face meeting can.

Community Building with Social Media

For help in synching your social networking sites, refer to this YouTube clip from eHow Tech: http://www.youtube.com/watch?v=hhUyw4nc5YQ.

The webinar *Using Social Media to Enhance School–Community Relations* was first aired on 22 March 2013. Educators Shawn Blankenship, Patrick Larkin, Michael Smith, and Dan Cox took part in it. You can find the webinar archived here: https://connect.uky.edu/p5xquedc2fe/?launcher=false&fcsContent=true&pbMode=normal.

If you want to start smaller than blogging, consider creating a Twitter account, a Facebook Fan Page for the school, or a Google+ Hangout, where you can post shorter status updates about what's happening at the school. You can post the results of the day's cross-country meet and parents can "like it" or even share it on their own Twitter feeds, or you can send a reminder about the School Council meeting in the resource center.

In fact, it is fairly easy to post one update and have it synched, or synchronized, to various forms of social media all at once. Your followers can then choose their favorite social media tool. For example, you can use a third-party app to synch Twitter, LinkedIn, Facebook, and WordPress (a popular, free blogging engine) simultaneously. These kinds of third-party apps emerge and are improved regularly (at time of writing, HootSuite is popular). A quick search on the YouTube website will yield a plethora of how-to videos to help you with any tech question, including how to synch your social media platforms.

Patrick Larkin won the National Digital Principal Award, given by the National Association of Secondary School Principals (NASSP), in 2012. A year later, he led the webinar *Using Social Media to Enhance School–Community Relations*. In the webinar, he noted these two powerful advantages of social media:

1. *Positive Public Relations* — Principals can take advantage of social media to share and promote the wonderful things happening at their schools with the world.

2. *Learning from One Another* — Schools could learn from one another if principals began to share their successful initiatives.

To put it differently, using social media can enable schools to reach a broader audience than that served by the immediate school community. In so doing, there can be a kind of pollination of energies and ideas.

Tips for principals using social networking sites

Establish the educational goals and set the tone. You will want to ensure that your teachers who use social media set clear educational goals and maintain their professional persona. What is the purpose of the social networking site (SNS)? What will the site be used for? What is the role of the teacher? What are the expectations for students in terms of responding? The guidelines for use must be specific, and you can model this by indicating your expectations in your initial post(s). Furthermore, although interacting on a social networking site can seem less formal than in the workplace, be sure to set the right tone by modeling what kinds of things to say, as well as how to say them. We recommend that principals and teachers use a formal, professional tone, as demonstrated in the blogs listed in "Inspiring Blogs to Follow," above.

Guide the discussion. When a social networking site is used to extend discussion on a topic, the quality of interaction may be shallow and bereft of any in-depth or critical thinking unless the site is set up and used properly. You can encourage positive interaction and promote constructive conversations through example. One way to do this is to pose questions in your own posts and to solicit comments or feedback. When someone responds to one of your posts, acknowledge it by continuing the conversation. Encourage your followers to think critically and to challenge your thinking about a topic, and be sure you disagree in an agreeable way. Stay away from negativity.

You cannot expect everyone to agree with your opinion. Sometimes, you may receive a post that creates awkward moments, but these can be powerful learning opportunities for everyone. If a follower makes a comment that is too personal or makes a negative statement about someone by name, for example, the way you handle the matter will be public. As author of the blog or Twitter feed, you have the right to delete a comment you deem inappropriate, but if you decide to respond publicly, be very careful about what you say. Remember that a social networking site facilitates an exchange of information in multiple directions!

Unless the platform allows the creator to approve content before it is posted, school leaders cannot control everything posted. We (the authors) regularly use social networking sites in our work with teachers and students. When a student posts something inappropriate (a photo, a comment, a video), we use it as a teachable moment to talk about netiquette and review the guidelines for use. We also maintain the ability to edit posts and have, on occasion, deleted an inappropriate addition. Instead of our avoiding the use of a social networking site with students, we help students learn how to use such sites ethically and responsibly.

Get connected. One real advantage of using a social networking site is the speed with which we can make relevant connections between school and world happenings. For example, if one of your school's initiatives is using iPads, you can link to relevant articles or YouTube video clips that talk about iPads in education.

Be committed. Once you begin using a social networking site, don't disappear. As a principal, you are very busy, but posting regularly and responding to others' posts in a timely way demonstrates commitment to your school community. Although you may want to delegate the posting of school news on the site to someone you trust, you should send any posts that express opinion yourself.

We conclude this chapter with a reminder for you, as a digital principal, to keep abreast of educational research into how digital media can enhance student learning — and be prepared to share what you find with your staff. Similarly, encourage teachers to look for confirmation that use of technology in education can support student achievement. They will find it. The interview below indicates how Principal Mike Whitmarsh mobilized the staff of a new school to embrace technology for the benefit of the students.

"Build It and They Will Come"
Interview with Principal Mike Whitmarsh

We caught up with Principal Mike Whitmarsh shortly before his retirement. In 2010, Mike was responsible for opening a technology-rich school that hosted 450 students and 31 staff members. We asked him these questions about his experiences there.

1. How do you ensure ongoing professional development in technology fluency and integration among your teachers within your school?

Build it and they will come. By providing the technology in a collaborative school culture of professional learning and with outstanding support by our Board's Individual Laptop Program courses, our staff were able to share and learn from each other.

2. How do you personally model effective communication and collaboration using digital-age tools?

I suggest to my staff that, if they want to see what I am communicating daily to our school community, they should frequently check our website and Twitter feed. [You can view the Twitter feed and website at http://whitbyshores.ddsbschools .ca. At the time the sample tweets appeared, about 650 tweets had been recorded, and there were 238 followers.]

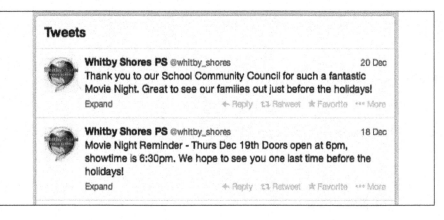

3. What do you do to stay abreast of emerging trends in technology in learning and current educational research?

Staying abreast of emerging trends . . . I ask my students and my son. I find CNET (or c/net) helpful. [CNET is a website that publishes reviews, articles, podcasts, and blog entries about digital technologies for consumers.]

4. How has technology enabled staff to promote character education?

Framed by our three big ideas — Caring for Others, Embracing Who We Are, and We Are All Interconnected — staff have moved to embedded character education in all they do, every minute of every day. Technology has allowed staff and students to move through learning to caring to action, both locally and globally. Engaged students who feel that they are making a difference perform better! Technology enables both staff and students.

Chapter 6 addresses further how technology enables action based on caring. There is also an appendix that provides a unit plan on raising students' consciousness about cyberbullying and how to prevent it. The unit plan involves students in at least seven activities that require them to explore the potential of digital technologies.

5

Purposeful Change for Systemic Improvement

The International Society for Technology in Education (ISTE) provides administrators with a standard for making systemic improvement. Check out ISTE Standards • A. www.iste.org/standards/standards-for-administrators.

The digital principal leads purposeful change in order to maximize student learning through the infusion and implementation of technologies. Deliberately designed change based on sound information permits the principal to make and maintain systemic improvement in the reaching of educational goals. The digital principal draws on and interprets a range of data about the school community, hires and supports staff in being able to work with technologies creatively and well, ensures a healthy infrastructure, and fosters strategic partnerships within and without the school community, all in aid of systemic improvement. Through acting in these ways, the digital principal exercises transformational leadership, which has demonstrated the most dynamic potential for administrative guidance of purposeful change.

Leading Purposeful Change

As first presented in Chapter 1, the style of leadership best suited to leading purposeful change is *transformational*. Leaders guide, rather than control their followers, motivating, communicating, and facilitating communication so that followers learn how to advance commonly held goals. They focus on developing personal relationships, paying attention and care to the needs of individuals, and providing ethical modeling of desired behaviors.

So, as a transformational leader, the digital principal motivates staff, students, parents, and other community members to work collaboratively towards the infusion of digital technologies. Achieving this depends in part on being well versed in school goals and familiar with the context of the school community. The transformational leader is then able to continually remind the school community of established school goals. As a facilitator, the digital principal promotes communication between members of the school community. This work includes acknowledging both successes and failures that teachers may experience in various efforts to incorporate digital technologies in the classroom. Without this communication, individual teachers cannot learn from the efforts of their peer community. This kind of sharing, as facilitated by the principal, reflects inter-agency cooperation; it thus acknowledges the importance of collective decision-making and contributions by others within the school and through community partnerships.

Successful day-to-day operations in the school are determined largely by the productive leadership of the administrative team. Development, communication, and implementation are essential components for administrator(s) to fulfill their leadership role within the school community. *Development* refers to the educational framework and policy, which enables purposeful change and innovation. Communication, whether by correspondence, modeling, or sharing resources and information, is the vehicle that directs change in the community. Under the digital principal, implementation of purposeful change is part of everyday management.

The School Community — Life Phase and Composition

The school community encompasses all school stakeholders, including students, staff, parents, and members of the greater community. Schaps (2003, p. 31) describes a viable school community as "caring, inclusive, participatory" for students. The digital principal is in touch with the nature and needs of the local community.

As you hold a leadership position, you will already have insight into the specific profile of your school community. Aspects include demographics, educational aims, goals established for educational achievement, and access levels to technology. Knowledge of the community composition will help you to define possible leadership roles and ways in which your school can aid the school community through technology. It might be through leading a seminar on Internet safety for parents, sharing through school e-letters news of upcoming fundraisers for school computer equipment, or announcing community events that celebrate the diversity of your school's population. Ways to promote the latter include making simple acknowledgments of holidays and customs, recognizing student achievements outside the school, and announcing school participation in sporting events and cultural concerts. Developing a school-and-community partnership plan that accounts for school and community needs will ensure that initiatives lead to success.

One useful exercise is the creation of a formal community profile.

Creation of a community profile

Profile Elements

- Ethnicity
- Language
- Household income
- Education

When thinking about a model for purposeful change, effective administrators consider demographic information about their school community. For example, administrators in the West Hill area of Toronto, Ontario, might use a 2006 City of Toronto demographic study.

The study shows that the local population includes a higher number of dependents (children and young people under 24 at 34 percent) with a larger population of immigrant families that do not speak a national language at home (roughly 20 percent) than the rest of Toronto. The West Hill area is populated by households where about 32 percent of families earned below $40 000 per year, 48 percent earned between $40 000 and $99 999 per year, and about 20 percent of families reported over $100 000 in annual family revenue. In addition, statistics on the composition of youth show a high number of immigrant youth (34.7 percent) and visible minority youth (62.9 percent). Further, 13.7 percent of people between 20 and 24 years of age reported that their high-school education was incomplete, which is more than 3 percent higher than the regional standard.

Administrators in West Hill, then, would identify such community characteristics as varied income levels with a concentration of middle-class families, a large number of visible minority and immigrant youth (English language learners, or ELLs), and a greater average of high-school dropouts than the norm.

When demographic factors are considered, the needs of the population are exposed. In the case of West Hill, questions like these would arise:

The *digital divide* is based on access to technology, including both the financial ability to obtain computers and the knowledge of the language and digital manipulation to support technology users.

- Which areas need additional English language support?
- Are there self-esteem initiatives in the community?
- Is there assistance to parents who may not have crossed the digital divide?
- Is there financial assistance or greater need of physical access to technology?
- Is there current research that can address student retention in school through technological initiatives?
- Is there a presence or absence of community resources (public libraries, community centres, post-secondary offerings) that help lessen the digital divide?

Up-to-Date Data Needed

Remember, though, that these sample demographics are not current and that many changes can occur. It is important to stay as current as possible in order to factor the most recent data into evolving plans.

These are all appropriate questions for administrators to take into account as they strive to engage the community. There will also be other questions that would help them decide on initiatives when considering school demographics. For example, questions relating to the effects of culture and assimilation would be important for administrators to consider as they plan for purposeful change.

Determination of life phase

Every school community is at some phase in a life cycle. Understanding the phases of change will give you a greater awareness of the history of your school community. The Centre for Innovative & Entrepreneurial Leadership (CIEL) uses a matrix that aptly describes what is meant by a community's life cycle, and we adopt it here. The matrix, which is in the public domain, presents four phases for identifying current trends in school-wide initiatives.

1. *Pre-community phase:* The school is in need of a leadership plan of action. A school in this phase is likely brand-new or undergoing a dramatic transformation, such as adopting a new curriculum.

2. *Emergence phase:* The school is in need of solutions to existing problems. Its focus is on short-term issues, such as behavior and expectations, and a lack of sustainable policy.

3. *Vision phase:* The school has reached a consensus on a plan of action. In this phase, the school uses community resources and interagency cooperation to build a viable, long-term plan for the future: one directed at such matters as curriculum, behavior management, student retention, and school policy.

4. *Actualization phase:* The school's actions are proven to be successful in the community. A school in this phase will have a developed sense of community, clear and attainable goals for the institution and its members, and the ability to learn from previous practices.

The CIEL matrix shows the evolution of the school community. The pre-community, or chaos, phase is characterized by a lack of development in the community. Resources are generally not shared in this phase as little value is placed in the established community; however, a community may still be formed through the action of a well-respected leader. In the emergence phase, a community does exist, but it has significant and pervasive problems. As a result, the school community is able to fulfill only the short-term needs of community members. School communities, then, can focus on ensuring that they meet these short-term goals to build trust and respect within them. The vision phase allows administrators to shift their focus to long-term goal planning. In this stage, members of the school community begin working together to identify community values and plan according to shared vision. Finally, in the actualization phase, the school community is highly developed. The digital principal is encouraged to learn more about the history and culture of school community members, and to understand what resources are readily shared. Growth at this stage is dependent upon ongoing critical reflection to maintain the gains achieved at each previous phase.

Each phase represents a critical assessment of the current school climate and thereby points to which action is under development. For example, in the chaos phase, there is a need for leadership to emerge; in the vision phase, the focus is on communication.

Achieving departmental cooperation within a school among subject-specialist teachers and lead grade teachers, as well as cooperation with educational support staff outside a school community, is essential to determining the school's life phase. Members of the school services team — educational psychologists, speech pathologists, social workers, guidance counsellors, teachers, and administrators — will have valuable insights into the school's internal communications. Although less involved in school operations and educational programming, stakeholders, such as afterschool-care providers, may also provide insight into the school's development phase. Other community stakeholders may be helpful, as well. These include charitable organizations, which may assist in developing the school's social justice goals; industries, such as school food services; organized sports groups; special interest groups, such as those pertaining to learning disabilities; and other special services for family support. Finally, coordinating efforts and making active comparisons with other schools in the same school board, district, or province/state will help to identify the school's life phase and provide others with opportunities for mentoring and leadership as a part of the developmental process.

The digital principal's role

The digital principal plays a key role in identifying the life phase, something that is crucial to development, as it facilitates a deeper understanding of how to approach purposeful change. Bettering the school community can be realized only by accurately identifying the current phase, resolving conflict, coming up with a vision and agreeing on how to achieve it, and then implementing that vision. The current state of affairs in the community is recognized.

The digital principal examines the underlying interactions between community members and organizations to accurately determine the community's lifecycle phase. In determining the phase, then, consider the following questions:

1. Is the population of your community homogeneous? How does your school population figure into the life cycle?
2. Are you engaging the needs and diversity of your community?
   Think about how community bulletin boards at local meeting places and public shopping areas portray what is happening in the community. For example, are there associations for new language learners or immigrants that provide language classes to which you could offer resource time for learners and tutors in your computer lab with students assisting? What about early

Potential Community Partners

Consider forming partnerships with any of the following groups and organizations:

- Community groups, such as Boys and Girls Club, YMCA, YWCA, and Rotary Club
- The local municipality
- Computer stores, bookstores, grocery stores
- Cultural organizations, such as art galleries and theatre companies
- Charities (e.g., United Way)
- Churches
- Youth outreach programs
- Association focused on learning disabilities
- Heath-related organizations

learning programs for young children? Could you offer a morning storytime in your school library for new families in the community? Arranging for students to volunteer at the food bank or work in community soup kitchens is another way to promote involvement.

Are opportunities for partnership available? Consider how the community might be able to offer them. What do you and your school hope to achieve? Is it to improve students' engagement and contribution in the community? to facilitate academic improvement and skill development through mentoring? to improve the social and health well-being of future young learners? How will community partnership be achieved?

3. How does your community use digital technologies? Consider where community members gain access to the Internet if not in their private homes. How can your school become familiar with public access to technology in places such as libraries, Internet cafés, and museums? Are there community members who are well suited to using technology? Consider how to draw on this type of expertise within your community to mentor your students to be better digital users. Understanding the issues around technology and access are important to you and your school community.

The Community Profile Through Various Lenses

In addition to creating the overall community profile, you can create a school profile. Two lenses by which others can see the school are the digital and the community lenses.

The digital lens

Create a digital lens from which your school could be viewed through digital platforms such as Twitter, Facebook, and blogs. For example, one school principal tweeted her school's progress to fundraise for a set of classroom tablets. Another placed an Animoto video on the school webpage with pictures of playground drawings and a student-devised wish list of playground equipment. Yet another used LinkedIn: after creating a profile, she found a group of school administrators of whom she could ask questions about digital platforms and fundraising, and discuss challenges that faced her school. Feedback from this online group helped the principal to understand how other principals perceived the school.

The community lens

Although using social media will promote understanding of your school, you will also need to build relationships with community members to increase their interest in the school. Your digital presence will be enhanced if you consider how membership could grow through your direct communication and involvement with the school community. Attending and representing your school in public meetings and projects can bring greater access to speakers and leaders with expertise: they may be able to offer mentoring or creative direction through their use of social media such as LinkedIn. Further partnering within the community, such as with a Boys and Girls Club or the neighborhood YMCA/YWCA, will build your school's profile. For example, we have seen a school and an afterschool program work as partners to select homework mobile apps to be used at the afterschool program to reinforce curricula, such as math facts.

An authoritative school profile

Letting your community view the school through both types of lenses — as an entity with both a community and a digital presence — ensures that the school profile reflects the diversity in how your school is viewed and its capacity to be involved in the community for the greater good.

For one of our research sites, we completed an overview of the types of community engagements in which school families took part. Many of the activities pointed to ways in which the school could mentor and become more involved in the community. For example, at a community afterschool program, we took note of the types of meetings offered, such as for parent groups and youth gatherings, as well as invitations to take part in other community groups. We also noted that the afterschool center had a computer room equipped with tablets sponsored by community businesses, suggesting an interest on the part of local businesses in promoting the well-being of community members. On the bulletin boards, we saw posters and news of community gatherings, most with webpage references: events ranged from harvest suppers to evenings of bingo. These notices encouraged us to think that the school would do well to invest further in the community.

Digitally strengthening your school's connections to its community is good practice. You can connect to your community through showing links to community events on the school webpage and by tweeting about your school's volunteer contributions to the community. Making such community observations, furthering digital connections with community groups, and acknowledging upcoming local events will help you, as leader, to develop an understanding of the community.

Of course, talking to stakeholders is paramount. Conducting surveys and collecting anecdotal information from the student body and staff, as well as making observations, will help you. This gathering of information will allow you to more fully understand and connect to the needs of your community.

Connecting with your community in person and using social media to build relationships will help enable others to perceive your school as a vibrant place for learning, worthy of involvement. Consider what happened after Principal Edward Vanguard led a workshop to engage teachers in using more social media networking to connect to their school community. Sharon Bannache, the school's literacy lead teacher in primary, explored use of Twitter to engage parents of the children in her class with experts on the importance of play-based learning in the home. Sharon began to follow and re-tweet concerns that some advocates had expressed through tweeting and social media about the decline of play in young children's lives. Through her posting of tweets describing learning moments gained through play in her Kindergarten classroom, parents began to understand how learning and play are connected at home.

Technology configuration inventory

Creating a technology configuration inventory involves thinking about how to represent your school profile within your school and community, appreciating how technology configures your school communications with your community, and understanding how various digital tools work.

Go on your site, and analyze its technological configuration by using the following steps:

1. Get the big picture. Make a list of all forms of community in which your school is involved (e.g., afterschool or community programs, school clubs, organizations) and the pertinent types of stand-alone tools (computers, digital devices, game systems). Think about why the tools are used and by whom. Where possible, list resources outside the school that can supplement this list.
2. Create a five-column table, using the headings below, to visually clarify the big picture. For each platform (second column from left), list the tools and note the ones being used. Why are some not being used? Are there duplicates? Are there issues related to integration between tools?
3. To the left of "Platform," make a note of which community activities or digital tools are used as support in your community.
4. To the right of "Stand-Alone Tools," identify the key features of tools. Are some of these features commonly or rarely used? What are the reasons for that?
5. Assess actual tool use. Identify which tools are dominant and which are used only by smaller groups and individuals.

Example of Technological Configuration Data Collection Table

Community Activities	Platform	Stand-Alone Tools	Key Features	Usage
Afterschool computer club; video game club; ESL digital support; home link websites	Twitter LinkedIn Facebook E-letter	26 computers, including desktop hardware, monitors, keyboard, and mouse	Internet access, numeracy and literacy software, school-wide subscription to TumbleBooks	After school, 10 students use computers. During school, some students must wait for computers.

An emerging picture of needed change

Now think back, and bring community profiles and technological configurations together. How do they inform each other? How is your school's profile configured through technology and presented to your community?

Think about what connections need to be strengthened and for what reasons. For example, are there areas of technological configuration that do not address the community profile? Have you considered including language support for new English language learners with websites to enhance oral language? It is important to review whether there is physical access to technology, such as a community center with a computer lab for public use. Further, consider the matter of parental support with regard to technology and how you can provide this to parents at school. Perhaps bring in a person from the community to teach skills but also to talk about safety on the Internet. At one community center, children and parents took part in a workshop, "Creating YOU on Facebook," led by a social media specialist, and parents also attended a session titled "Understanding the New Universe of Cyberspace." Such workshops are a great way to find out what parents and students need and to connect and enhance your digital profile.

Following through on a larger and more integrated picture demonstrates how you, as a digital principal, can move forward. Pause and consider the following.

1. *How will particular resources allow you and your staff to accomplish your collective goals?* For example, what if you, with input from your teachers, decide to choose one software instruction program because it is accompanied by a parent-and-home-support website? You will have to assess whether it will be used at home and to what extent. Consider, too, whether the software can be used by a child without constant parent support.

2. *How will the school acquire technology?* Once you and your staff have established which resources are most suitable to your community's profile, you will need to determine how to acquire and implement use of your school's technology. Planning over a three-year period, welcoming staff input, and considering school needs will lead to a more cohesive plan. Some schools decide on a school-wide plan with early grade goals, skills, and software to be used each year.

3. *How will you address changes in technology and pedagogy?* Once you have thought about the questions above, move forward with a plan, actively considering how and what you will change to accommodate technological development and emerging pedagogical approaches.

Thinking about how you will upgrade and address changes for the classroom will help you to make major decisions. Introducing use of an interactive whiteboard in all classrooms, for example, may require a technological component of professional development for your staff. Invite other technology teachers and digital principals within your school board to come and share their expertise. For example, on a professional development day, high-school principal Ed Hardy and his school's technology teacher gave a workshop at Sunnyside Elementary, a newly opened school, on the basics of using interactive whiteboards. Three whiteboards were placed around the room, and the teachers from the home school as well as from other schools practiced the skills demonstrated in the workshop. By the end of the session, the teachers had shared contact information, and both Ed and the technology teacher had made plans to visit another school to assist in training. As a parallel, a public librarian was invited into one of our research schools to talk to students about how to evaluate a good app for their tablets.

Promotion of the Digital Initiative

School leadership in innovation entails motivating the school community to take active part in new technology initiatives. You can promote your digital initiative by recognizing those individuals who strive to use technology in the school in a positive and useful way. Innovative technological leaders may be experienced teachers showing sound teaching methods through the use of technology, and new teachers who strive to address multiple learning styles using new digital tools.

There are many ways to recognize these leaders among staff. You could adopt token systems, such as a small gift; provide a symbol or representation of leadership, such as an award; or make school-wide mention of success. This recognition may be more effective when it is promoted within the school community and offered to a person who shares electronic educational resources or provides direction in the use or assessment of digital resources. Constant attention to innovation programs (recognition of staff leaders, professional development, and school-wide development), as well as ongoing assessment of those programs, is essential to successful implementation of technology in schools.

In addition to positive reinforcement of your digital initiative plan, consider adopting a motto to deliver your initiative school-wide — the examples in the margin are typical. Using popular culture references (perhaps from a song, video game, or movie) may help you attract student attention.

Encourage students to develop a motto, through the use of a poster campaign within your school, or plan a school assembly to showcase student digital projects (such as robotics, videos, and digital music). Approaching innovation in educational curriculum and professional development with enthusiasm is the primary step to stewarding technology-related programs and integrating innovation into the curriculum.

Monitoring Implementation Through Evaluation

Collecting and analyzing data on student performance and participation will help in determining whether the innovation initiative is having a positive impact. For example, at one school, the technology teacher was key to implementing a school-wide questionnaire about digital skills. In particular, she asked students to note what type of computer, mobile phone, or tablet they used; what social network sites and websites they and their families frequented; and the types of schoolwork they completed at home and the programs used. Students were also asked to describe their creative endeavors and to identify the programs related to them (e.g., iPhoto and GarageBand). It was found that students were quite engaged in technology in their home lives. In particular, social networking sites, such as Facebook, and photo-sharing sites, such as Flickr, were mentioned frequently. It was determined that students had adequate digital access through either home or through other family members and friends.

When students complete self-assessments or technological profiles, the data can provide a useful supplement to the school profile and technological configuration profiles.

Ways to Measure the Success of an Initiative

Consider the following options:

1. *Teacher Technology Profile:* With the introduction of new technologies, ask staff to self-assess their knowledge of, level of comfort with, and practical use of digital tools. What tools do they use every day? For what purpose? What areas need improvement? How does this relate to current and future professional development? Did this change or improve over the course of the year?

2. *Student self-assessment:* Digital surveys and handwritten student questionnaires are intended to measure the success of school-driven initiatives. Remember to have a representative sample, such as more than 30 respondents. Provide both paper and digital assessments, and include an opportunity for participants to share their own concerns. Administering the survey at beginning or end of term or both is a good idea and will let you gauge any changes in attitudes or thoughts

Sample Phrases for Success
Above and Beyond the Call of Duty
Educating Students for Success in a Changing World
Preparing Students for Success in a Changing World
The Future Begins Here!

A Teacher Technology Profile is provided as an appendix. Depending on your own context and purposes, you can adapt it for your school's particular context or use only part of it.

on the use of technology at your school. Be sure to include questions on school versus home use, new skills learned, application to course curricula (such as career education and language arts), and areas that students would like to improve (such as education in current technology trends, including robotics and animoto). Consider making the questionnaires private so that students can provide candid answers for maximum effect.

Sample Questionnaire

1. Do you use the Internet at home or in another place, such as a library or at the home of a relative or friend?
2. How often do you use the Internet at home or in other places? (Daily, once a week, monthly)
3. What technology devices do you use at home or in other places to gain access to the Internet?
4. Out of 100 percent, how much of the above time indicated do you use the Internet for school projects?
5. Provide a list of what you use the Internet for at home, using any of the devices (or others) mentioned above.
6. Provide a list of the top five Internet sites that you use for school projects.
7. If you use social networking sites to stay connected, identify which ones. Do you connect with friends from school on them?
8. Give a detailed example of how you use these social networking sites. (Example: To stay connected to people, to set meeting times, to comment on other peoples' thoughts and pictures.)
9. What types of designing or creative things do you do on the Internet? What do you enjoy the most when using the Internet? (Perhaps watching YouTube videos, socially connecting with others, gaming.)
10. In your opinion, could we teach school better by using the types of websites or creative things you do on the Internet? If you think yes, then provide an example of how a school lesson could be better taught using one of these.

Surveys given online have many qualities that make them popular to use. For example, they can provide immediate feedback to help you inform your programming. They are a way to engage your students in a conversation on issues in the school. Further, they can be completed anonymously while enabling you to gather information on the needs of your community. For example, you may wish to provide a survey to gauge student interest in social justice issues and causes to find out which causes the student body may want to support through school-wide fundraising. Schools can also administer surveys to parents as a way of finding out the different types of technology, forms of access, and technological knowledge parents have. Data gathered in such surveys is helpful to developing parent workshops and providing supports and information through school e-letters.

Two online tools, SurveyMonkey and Wufoo, can be used to find out what students think about such matters as use of and attitudes on the use of social media for social justice causes. As we know from our research use of them, both of these tools provide easy access and can be placed on your school website or your school's Facebook page. Internet surveys extend your access to a larger audience in your community and permit faster distribution. Because the surveys are easy to construct due to the friendly tools, you can engage particular audiences for response, such as parents of one grade level or parents of children taking part in a particular sport. You can also use the surveys as needed, perhaps engaging parents on issues facing the School Council. Often, comments provided could lead you and your school to new opportunities and avenues to explore: these could pertain to fundraising, community involvement, or new curricular opportunities for students.

Easy reporting of the data in spreadsheet form makes analysis quite simple. When data are in this form, you can look at categories, see building trends, and consider how best to engage your school community in discussing the findings. For example, you could share the results through posting on the school website, perhaps using summary data tools as provided by SurveyMonkey and Wufoo. Making the results available through emails to survey respondents is a good idea, as well. Surveys given at the school can build collaboration between the school and community. Parent and students feel a part of the decision-making process, which leads to more active engagement on the part of all stakeholders.

Recruiting and Retaining Digitally Competent Staff

A key role for the digital principal and administrative team, including tech staff, is promotion of professional learning opportunities that focus on innovation and infusion of digital technologies to enhance student learning.

It is, of course, important both to recruit teachers who have experience using technology and to retain staff who are digitally competent. Teachers who have an expertise in technology tend to take responsibility for allocating the time and necessary resources, and for promoting professional development among other staff members, as well as integrating technology in their classrooms. Tech staff and the digital principal may find it productive to work together on planning, and to both facilitate and take part in professional learning communities or collegial circles that support staff in the new use of digital technologies. This approach may be achieved through the design of professional development programs offered through school district workshops. It is also important that the principal and tech staff model effective ways of collaborating and communicating with colleagues who are using digital technologies in the classroom. Finally, like the digital principal, tech staff must remain well versed in trends in the uses of digital technologies for promoting student learning in the classroom.

Potential interview questions for tech new hires

Below is a list of questions that administrators may pose to teaching applicants to determine their level of proficiency and comfort with using digital technologies in the general classroom. These questions are not meant to replace a comprehensive consideration of an applicant's teaching credentials and experience. The desired responses will vary according to the needs that the digital principal is striving to meet.

1. How have you used, or plan to use, technology in the classroom? Please give an example.

2. What is your educational philosophy on technology? For example, do you believe in one-to-one support, computers as classroom centers, or technology as a dedicated subject area only? Please explain why.
3. How can you support technology-driven initiatives in the school? How would you involve hesitant or uninterested staff in using technology?
4. What do you feel are important trends in educational technology?
5. What are your qualifications regarding technology? For example, what professional development and education do you have in the area? What technologies are you familiar with? Do you have any expertise? What is it?

How the digital principal helps to promote technology in the classroom

As this book has shared, with the abundance of technology out there to master, you cannot learn everything. Here are a few things you can do as you rethink the best strategies to use for accessing technology and the desired expertise that might benefit your staff, school, and parents.

- Focus on systemic improvement, where you provide leadership as a means to increase organization through the use of digital technologies in the school.
- Put an emphasis on purposeful change to ensure the achievement of the digital technology learning goals that you establish.
- With other educational administrators, collaborate to collect and analyze data that may increase both staff performance and student learning.
- Recruit personnel who are highly competent in implementing and using digital technologies and whose involvement will facilitate the attainment of learning goals.
- Consolidate partnerships to ensure the supports necessary to achieve systemic improvement overall.
- Develop and maintain an infrastructure that is supportive of teaching and learning with digital technologies.

Facilitating implementation by the classroom teacher

Below is a list of recommendations to facilitate the implementation of technology by teachers in the classroom. It is up to the digital principal to coordinate and work with staff to determine how best to implement them. The facilitating phase requires you to think about how to motivate your staff to become a part of the implementation process. For monthly staff meetings at Barrington Elementary School, for example, the principal invites a staff member to introduce a new website that has been used in the teacher's classroom. This exercise engages all staff members in a collegial circle of learning and discussion of how the website could be used to achieve particular grade curriculum outcomes. Added value to this approach is an opportunity for staff to mentor. Further to this, perhaps to reinforce the proposed purchase of a classroom set of tablets or e-readers, recommendations from presenters can be included in the school development plan given to School Council, disseminated to teachers through an email, or posted online in a professional learning community.

Recognizing the key role that staff will play in all phases of the facilitation process is always important. A great digital leader understands that the purchase of software and computer equipment is just the stepping-stone to technology access. The following list outlines how vital staff and technology expertise aids in building a school with digital technologies as part of the foundation.

- Teachers can model appropriate use of digital technologies with regard to the ethical, legal, and social issues often around the social media use of technology. (See Chapter 6.)
- Teachers can acknowledge that equitable access to digital resources is important for meeting the needs of all learners in an emerging digital culture and ensure that this possibility is met to the best abilities of the school.
- Teachers can promote the development of cultural understanding, as well as foster involvement in global issues, through the use of access provided by communication and digital technologies.

Developing Strategic Partnerships with Stakeholders

Establish open communication on technology-driven initiatives at your school by connecting with parents/guardians, students, and staff, both online and in person. Beyond that, promote parent–teacher interactions about your school's digital initiatives, making use of the school website, newsletter, phone calls, and notes home. Invite families to engage in conversations with their child's teacher, tech staff, or administration. Correspondence can be electronic, written, or personal.

If your research indicates a digital divide within the school community, take note of how you can help school members overcome this challenge. What public stakeholder supports can you find for your school? Stakeholders may include libraries, community groups, local government, local business, media groups, even larger telecommunication companies. Ways to help close the digital divide within your school community include these: sharing various links on your school webpage; providing information though your school newsletter on stakeholder contacts such as the public library, which may offer free wireless access and a laptop loan program; and pursuing a school grant program with telecommunication companies such as Rogers.

Resources for Civic Engagement

Elections Canada provides educational resources for teachers at the elementary and secondary levels, as well as for English as a second language and low literacy classes. These products and resources are designed to promote an increased interest in civic engagement through voting in the classroom.
http://www.elections.ca/content.aspx?section=vot&dir=yth/tea&document=index&lang=e

Tapping Community Resources

Elementary teacher Tina Roche partnered with community members to bring rich learning experiences to her classroom. To begin this year-long initiative, she invited into the classroom a parent who had worked in the local provincial government as the municipal chair for elections. The parent showed the children a government department website which illustrated, on a Google map, the different electoral districts in the province. Children asked questions about the voting process, including some on the setup of polling booths, counting of votes, and what happens in the event of a tie between candidates.

Digital divide versus civic engagement

Tina's Grade 5 class then followed the campaigns of two municipal candidates running for mayor in the capital city of St. John's: one tweeted and the other did not use Twitter. For some children, this was their introduction to Twitter; they understood the microblog's ability to send messages to many people at once.

The children were well informed of each candidate's election platform and were surprised by the outcome of the election. It raised an opportunity for Tina to discuss how different social media platforms are followed by particular demographic groups, some of which may not use their vote. She was also able to address the digital divide, noting that not everyone has access to the type of campaign blogging used by the one candidate.

Fostering of community connections

This experience inspired Tina to continue exploring how social media are being used within the school community. For example, as a community partner with the school, the local Boys and Girls Club established a Facebook group to help keep members and the community connected.

Here are some ideas to keep in mind.

- Encourage trust-building initiatives within the community to strengthen the connections. For example, there could be a guideline that teachers strive to make timely responses to emails from parents and students. Such guidelines serve to establish for the community your trust in their thoughts and communication. They also reinforce the importance of technology in the community.
- Establish guidelines for engagement in online forums, including appropriate behavior. This effort may include the development of netiquette for students to follow (see Chapter 6 for more on netiquette).
- Recognize the potential of using digital software and social media to help people reach common goals and objectives related to fostering a sense of local, national, and global community and citizenship.
- Maintain a balance between online and offline personal relationships. In particular, encourage students to see that relationships may be fostered both online and offline at the same time. For example, children who play at school during recess and lunch could meet online to play video games on the weekends with parental and guardian permission.

Adoption of the guidelines above allows students and teachers to participate in the development of healthy and successful virtual communities. A *successful virtual community* is defined through user contributions to growth and maintenance, regular participation by members in that community, and a communal identity established by the frequent interaction and shared vision of members.

Ways to communicate and connect digitally with various stakeholders

- Develop afterschool digital programs or computer clubs. Doing so will increase access for those who have socio-economic challenges to technology.

  Creating an afterschool club for computer or digital programs will increase students' awareness of various computer safety skills. It will also offer access to those who lack access to this type of technology at home. At many local afterschool programs and public libraries, access to technology provides many opportunities, such as learning technology how-to skills.

Burke and Marsh's (2013) edited collection shares a number of research studies discussing friendships and relationships maintained online and offline by young learners while playing in virtual worlds, such as Club Penguin, Webkinz, and Stardoll.

- Promote homework sites, class blogs, and student websites to help ensure open and transparent communication about all classroom activities and expectations.

    With technology today, many people would rather be informed of what is happening in the classroom through the Internet. If parents or family members are checking their email, it is just as easy for them to be informed through homework sites, class blogs, e-letters, and student websites as it is to send letters home.

- Encourage teachers to accept virtual or electronic submissions, and encourage electronic communications about student work.

    Electronic submissions allow easier grading of students' work because issues of legibility and readability are drastically diminished. They also offer the potential for faster return.

- Invite teachers to explore the potential of virtual lectures or podcasts to capture class lessons.

    This approach embraces the diverse ways in which students learn, as the varying needs of visual and auditory learners are addressed. It also allows for students to review instructional material.

- Promote use of mobile messaging or tweeting to connect to parents about school events or assignments or even school closures due to extreme weather.

Criteria and values for connecting digitally

When administrators, teachers, parents or guardians, and students connect digitally, whether inside or outside the classroom, it is important that they do so responsibly. As educational leaders, we are each called to do the following, while being aware that there may be financial challenges to school and community resources.

- Maintain open minds and educate ourselves on digital practices through collaborating with colleagues and referring to educational resources, such as appropriate books, websites, and journals.
- Realize the importance of information and communications technologies (ICT) and their influence on learning. Keep in mind how this is a new learning experience for everyone.
- Provide adequate educational website support to guardians and parents. One way is to offer access to educational websites such as BrainPop, which has animated curricular content, through the school website (the school may be required to buy a licence). Often, children can access these programs during lunch hour and after school in computer clubs. Some schools encourage families to access school websites at home in their spare time or to take up the programs offered at school libraries. The availability of a free public service, such as that in libraries or museums, gives digital support.
- Use technological strategies with stakeholders in order to communicate efficiently and connect digitally within your communities. For example, use Facebook or Twitter feeds as a strategy to reach parents. Emailing parents with updates also works.
- Implement and adhere to adequate digital technological models for funding digital projects and supporting new technology.

To help foster adoption of the above criteria and values in our online communities, we can recognize and use opportunities to interact with stakeholders and communicate in person, as well. We could discuss in formal spaces (e.g., staff room, school resource center) and in informal spaces (e.g., public library, coffee shops — anywhere else we meet regularly to share experiences). With digital access, the school has a greater opportunity to develop, foster, and fine-tune relationships within the school community.

Creating and Maintaining a Technology Infrastructure

The digital principal takes a thorough approach to determining existing technological infrastructure and its current uses by students in order to better predict future needs and trends. With the technology teacher or committee, the principal documents current technology resources in the school. This information can be obtained by completing a technology inventory for each classroom. Ensuring that every classroom has the common technology it needs to satisfy the requirements of its grade and of the subject teacher intent on meeting curriculum outcomes is one way to promote equity. The digital principal also ensures that the library, art room, music room, laboratories, and designated skills–based rooms, such as for auto mechanics, have the technology they need for curricular purposes.

Pine Ridge District School Board
Technology Inventory — Hardware

School: <u>Pinecrest Elementary</u> Location/Room: <u>126</u> Date: ------------<u>2013</u>

Description	Model Number	Serial Number	Details	Cost	Purchase Date	Comments
MacBook Air	11 inch 256GB	AP 17346	1.3GHz 4GB	$1,199	June 2013	From SC funding
iPad	Mini Wi-Fi	P2639257	Retina Display 32GB	$519	Jan 2013	Shared with Room 130
iPad	Mini Wi-Fi	M211362	Retina Display 32GB	$519	Jan 2013	Shared with Room 130
Smart Board	SB-#10 WES	SB680-R2-864289	680i3	$3,300	July 2012	Moved from Room 125
Epson Projector	EX7220 Wirelss	B012BH 1865550	V11H55-2020	$499.96	July 2012	Bulb replaced Nov 2013

Inventory of technology for an elementary classroom

You can further assess the needs of your school by asking each teacher to complete a Teacher Tech Inventory, much like that on the next page.

Teacher Tech Inventory

Classroom # _____   Date _____

Classroom Computers

List the number of classroom computers and tablets _____ e-book readers _____
Do all classroom computers, tablets, and e-readers have Internet access?   Yes   No
Which ones have access? What about the type of access?

Devise a list of software and apps on the classroom computers:

Other Access to Technology in the School

Do your students visit a computer lab?   Yes   No
If yes, how often? _____

List the software titles on the lab computers:

List the websites and platforms for which your school has a subscription.

Do your students have access to the following equipment?
    A mobile laptop lab   Yes   No
    AlphaSmarts   Yes   No
    Hand-held devices (iPods, smartphones, tablets)   Yes   No
    Digital still cameras   Yes   No
    Digital video cameras   Yes   No
    Video-conferencing equipment   Yes   No
    Interactive whiteboard   Yes   No

Are students able to start work on lab computers and complete the work
on classroom computers, and vice versa?   Yes   No

Pembroke Publishers ©2014 *The Digital Principal* by Janette Hughes, Anne Burke ISBN 9781-55138-288-3

An *AlphaSmart* functions like a laptop computer but is strictly for word processing; it is therefore much like a digital typewriter. It works well in classrooms for students with special needs.

Smart Boards and Promethean boards are interactive whiteboards. Which is better for your school depends, of course, on your needs; however, Smart Boards need only finger or pen, not a special stylus, and are dominating the market. If purchasing, a school should come to a consensus on which board to adopt. Training resources are currently available for both.

Ways to address the funding challenge

One persistent challenge that administrators face is securing consistent and adequate funding to support technology infrastructure. While district school boards have increased their technology budgets over the years, there is still never enough money to go around. What are some practical ways of addressing this issue? Here are a few ideas to consider.

☐ Cut your textbook budget. Many publishers are moving to e-books. In particular, novels purchased as e-books are much cheaper than print copies, and they do not get lost or damaged.

☐ Go paperless. Post your school newsletter online and use a Twitter feed to make announcements to students or parents. These tweets can include 140-character reminders of upcoming school events. For example, Spring Hill Public School often tweets about recycling: "Recycling drop off tomorrow @ Spring Hill curb side 8:00 a.m. We hope to see you there!"

As much as possible, have teachers provide students with digital copies of handouts as PDFs or documents online, via their websites. Encourage teachers to show their students how to manage the documents on the computer. The goal here is to engage in a paperless curriculum where feasible, building the digital skills that students will need.

☐ At the junior- and senior-high levels, encourage the use of online agendas or calendars rather than purchasing these for students or subsidizing them.

☐ Encourage the use of interactive content rather than worksheets (see "Virtual Field Trips," below).

☐ Allow and encourage students to use their own mobile devices and laptops — Bring Your Own Device (BYOD). If students lack access to personal devices, give them priority for access to the digital technologies made available by the school.

☐ Whenever possible, encourage teachers to use freeware, free software, and the Cloud for storing and sharing.

☐ Collaborate with School Council and get help with fundraising. Involve other community members such as small businesses and parents, as well.

Virtual Field Trips

As part of promoting interactive experiences instead of worksheet use, encourage teachers to implement virtual field trips. These field trips can be used as an important complement to classroom learning that addresses the various ways of knowing for students. Here is a sampling of trips that classes can take as a way to journey and learn together as a community. Students can gain exposure to places without incurring the costs of visiting them in person.

- Global Trek (Geography):
  http://teacher.scholastic.com/activities/globaltrek
- Google Lit Trips (English Language Arts, History):
  Document3http://googlelittrips.com/GoogleLit/Home.html
- Le Louvre (Art, History):
  http://www.louvre.fr/en/visites-en-ligne
- Mount Everest (Geography):
  http://www.airpano.com/360Degree-VirtualTour.php?3D=Everest-Nepal

- Smithsonian, National Museum of Natural History [U.S.] (Natural Science, History):
  http://www.mnh.si.edu/panoramas
- Panoramas of the World (Geography, Natural and Social Sciences, History):
  http://www.360cities.net
  http://www.panoramas.dk/7-wonders/
- Space (Astronomy):
  http://quest.nasa.gov/vft

Technology grants

School leaders or even teachers can apply for technology grants. Many websites share information on where to apply and how to secure grants for technology in classrooms. These grants may be provided through government funding or non-profit organizations. Administrators and teachers need only conduct a simple Internet search to identify grants being offered in their area. One way to attract donors is to use your website to reach out to such individuals. Incorporate information such as your vision for your school, the demographics of your school and neighbourhood school population, and goals for your school; share pictures of successful fundraising and how donors have helped the school in the past.

Depending on the type of grant, you may have to fill in an application form or, more likely, write a detailed proposal in which you provide answers to important questions such as these:

- How will the technology be used to enhance collaboration between the school and community?

  Discuss how the school will engage with the donor to build a partnership that will aid others in the community. Perhaps a donation of tablets could be used by both the school and a community afterschool program.
- Who will be using the technology — numbers, grades, context? Do the students have special needs?

  Share a project that describes in detail the students and grade levels that will benefit.
- What technology is needed, and what does the specific technology you want to purchase afford students?

  Explain how students' lives could change outside school with access and opportunity to use such technology.
- How does the use of the technology align with local curriculum standards?
- How will you assess student progress in meeting both technology standards and content objectives?

  Share how a student's education is related to real-life skills through instruction using a particular device or piece of software.
- How will you evaluate the effectiveness of your initiative?

  Sharing an outline of what you hope to achieve for students through a grant or donation is ideal. You could present this in the implementation phase. For example, share a monthly calendar schedule on how a class set of tablets or iPads could be used at each grade level and identify the types of apps or online programming in which the children will engage.
- How will you disseminate your findings to colleagues at the school, district, and community levels?

Dissemination is about accountability. How will others see how the grant served the school and community? Will you share in a school assembly with the parents how children learned through technology? Will workshops be conducted on your project so that others can benefit from professional development?

- How sustainable is your initiative? Will you be able to use the technology in subsequent projects? Will you be able to use it in different ways?

Often, granting agencies ask how the learning will carry through after a project is completed. Will you repeat the project or seek further funding from others to extend the project? The idea here is that initial grant donations will lend more opportunity for learning and growth.

The line master on the next page can be given to teachers as a way of reminding them of the kind of approach to take to the use of technology in their classrooms.

A Holistic Action Checklist for Using Technology in the Classroom

☐ Take a holistic approach. Use technology to help students acquire new digital skills, not simply to engage their attention or provide a distraction. Have a purpose to using technology. Think about what you want students to learn to do with the technology and the programming around your curriculum. Remember to connect holistic approaches to the child, and promote learning within all facets of a child's life.

☐ Engaging in technology always affords opportunities for children to develop life skills. Remember, though, that technology in the classroom relies on the school having enough connectivity for students to engage on an equal footing.

☐ Is everyone of much the same understanding? Can you clearly communicate to your school community why you are using that particular technological tool in your lesson, your course, your classroom, with your students?

☐ What are you using the technology for? Technological education is not a replacement for teacher-centered learning; it is a means of engaging students in constructivist and multimodal approaches to learning.

☐ Address the matter of student safety. Help students realize the dangers in actions such as accessing inappropriate content, conducting illegal activity, and making unauthorized purchases or downloads on school machines. Educate your students on dangers associated with using technology, and make expectations and policies transparent in the appropriate use of technology.

☐ Understand the features of different digital tools. For example, laptops provide user monitoring and control that are not features of portable devices like tablets; tablets and phones are equipped with portable video-making capabilities not available on laptops. Think about what you are trying to achieve, and choose the most appropriate tool for a given task.

☐ Know the security and privacy risks associated with technology. Digital tools need to be protected by usernames and passwords in order to prevent confidential or personal information from being shared unwillingly.

☐ Remember that technology does not replace hands-on or real-world experience. What it can do is to augment the real-world learning of a child in wonderful ways.

☐ Connect online, make use of the wealth of information on the Internet, and share the great learning for students with critical skills that will assist them in their future digital journeys.

Pembroke Publishers ©2014 *The Digital Principal* by Janette Hughes, Anne Burke ISBN 9781-55138-288-3

6

Digital Citizenship

As digital technologies are infused into the school, there evolves a certain culture and with that, a sense of citizenship within that culture. The digital principal is intent on guiding that evolution and the way in which citizens — teachers, students, parents, and other stakeholders — deal with one another and people beyond. As a transformational leader, the digital principal sees the potential of technologies not only for addressing learning needs but for involving students in global issues — opening up the world through communication and collaboration tools.

The digital principal recognizes that citizenship always comes with responsibilities. Through modeling and promotion, the school leader helps teachers and students understand the social, ethical, and legal issues that arise from the creation of a digital culture. Online participants need to learn how to treat each other with respect and honesty, and also how to protect themselves from users who exploit the constraints of technologies. The digital principal facilitates policies and protocols on the safe, legal, and ethical use of technologies and information for the school community to follow. All efforts to promote positive digital citizenship are founded on there being equitable access to appropriate tools and resources: the digital principal strives to realize this.

The International Society for Technology in Education (ISTE) provides administrators with a standard for fostering digital citizenship. Check out ISTE Standards • A. www.iste.org/standards/standards-for-administrators.

What Is Digital Citizenship?

As administrators, we understand that the professional development of teachers and the teaching of students in the appropriate use of technology in schools is the cornerstone of digital citizenship education. Indeed, *education in digital citizenship* can be defined as "learning to use technology in an appropriate manner." This educational emphasis is especially critical as it relates to the misuse of technology, something that encompasses cyberbullying, downloading music illegally, and using cellphones during class. Three key questions for administrators to consider are these:

- How can we address any student and teacher abuse of technology?
- How do we extend current policies to cover digital practices in the school community?
- And how do these policies extend to promote education in digital citizenship, encompassing communication, understanding, and personal involvement?

"Digital citizenship involves the appropriate use of all current digital technologies (e.g., handheld computers, cell phones, laptops) as well as technologies that are still in development."
— Ribble and Bailey, 2007, p. 107

Nine elements of digital citizenship

According to Ribble and Bailey (2007), there are nine elements of digital citizenship for principals and other educational administrators to consider. These are identified below, with related questions posed.

1. **Access:** How can administrators ensure that all students and teachers have access to computers and other digital technologies? Can this access extend outside school hours?

2. **Commerce:** What kind of educational programming about online purchasing, choice of safe sites, and consumer education for online money management can be provided to high-school students and teachers? What forum(s) is most appropriate for this type of education? Is it the classroom, a subject, an afterschool group, an online opportunity, or something else?

3. **Communication:** First, let's think about how we as administrators use digital devices for conversation and for conveying information in our daily activities (e.g., email, texting, and blogging). How can we model and inform socially responsible digital communication to the school community? When is it inappropriate to use technology to communicate? What policies address the misuse of digital communication? What are the important issues regarding advantages and disadvantages of digital communication?

4. **Literacy:** Administrators need to be aware of how teachers are using technology in the classroom and how the use of digital devices is enhancing student learning. Are students being taught to use technology? Do teachers use technology to connect to curriculum-driven outcomes? Is there a detriment to using technology — or does technology replace or enhance non-digital practices in a meaningful way? For example, how can administrators ensure that teachers are using Smart Boards effectively? (Through professional development.)

5. **Etiquette:** How can administrators provide information and education about responsible digital communication, such as educational policy on the use or misuse of digital devices? What practices, policies, or promotional materials encourage critical thinking about proper use of cellphones and Facebook (for students and teachers), for example, and how that communication affects others in the community inside and outside school?

6. **Law:** The educational administration is responsible for the clear delivery of school policy on provincial/state and federal laws that pertain to the legal use of technology. Ongoing issues, such as "pirating" music or movies, copyright, and plagiarism, can and should be addressed in the school community. How can administrators prevent and discourage illegal use of technology? What can be done when illegal digital activities are reported in schools? What education is offered in the school to promote awareness of digital law?

7. **Rights and Responsibilities:** Expectations that students and staff will behave ethically when using digital technologies entail clear communication of digital rights and responsibilities. How can administrators raise awareness on key issues, such as cyberbullying and age-appropriate materials on websites? What other issues can be related to personal value systems or behaviors in digital forums?

8. **Health and Wellness:** Promotion of physiological and psychological wellness is essential to the school environment, so how can administrators identify and address dangerous technological practices, such as video game violence

or excessive playing, and their effects, which may include social withdrawal, inactivity, or physical strain due to computer height or placement?

9. **Security:** How can educational administrators promote and ensure that online safety practices are employed in school? Protection of personal information is important for both staff and students; digital protection from viruses for all school hardware, software, and networks is also important. In what ways can schools address the education of students and staff in safe digital communication? (The means include the nondisclosure of personal information, the installation of anti-virus software, and precautions taken against identity theft.) What can administrators do to promote personal safety when students and staff are communicating with others online?

Addressing the Issue of Digital Access

Digital access consists of more than securing access to computers and devices for students and teachers. It encompasses equal access to electronic communication for all school community members, including those who have physical disabilities, special needs, or socio-economic challenges.

The school administration faces the task of narrowing any digital divide (the economic disparity between those who have physical access to digital resources, as well as the knowledge and capacity to use them, and those who don't). Common causes of low digital access include low family finances (socio-economic causes); (dis)abilities and level of education (individual status causes); Internet speed and number of computer units available (physical location causes), such as rural areas not having high-speed access. Thinking about the specific needs of your school community is important in identifying whether there is a digital divide and how to address the issue of digital access.

How can we as administrators promote equal digital access? There are two levels of consideration: (1) the skill level (critical thinking, education, and leadership) and (2) the resource level (hardware and software, Internet service provider, and modifications for accommodations).

According to Ribble and Bailey (2007), there is a need to develop policies aimed at promoting "open computer labs, evening access to school libraries, and extracurricular activities . . . to make up the difference" (p. 14). When implementing such policies, the digital principal ensures that staff members are on board and available to supervise and facilitate access to these programs. Our experience working in schools suggests that staff are engaged and interested in offering wider access to students to help them gain more success. Keeping the computer lab open during lunch and after school is a common practice.

Recognizing public libraries as Wi-Fi hot spots

Are the quality and quantity of digital resources at your school sufficient to meet the needs of an ever-expanding digital education landscape? If you can answer yes, your school is fortunate; however, that may not be the case. So, how can you, as a principal, address the issue of equal digital access for students and families? Public libraries may provide a satisfactory answer.

Community libraries across Canada have risen to the challenge of providing digital access to their communities through various programs and resources. By working with your local community library, you may be able to expand access for children and their families in a way not feasible with your school's own supplies.

First thing to consider is simple access to computers and the Internet. Although the Internet seems to be everywhere, access to it remains out of reach for some. As education turns towards digital technologies, it is essential to the success of digital education to ensure that students have access to the technologies. Most public libraries have computers available for use by anyone with a library card. They also offer free Wi-Fi access to visitors, either parents or students, who have devices of their own (e.g., laptops, tablets, wireless-enabled e-readers, and smartphones). In most provinces, including Newfoundland and Labrador, there is a library network of publicly accessible Wi-Fi hot spots.

Sharing your school initiatives with the local library will allow the library to become part of your community effort to increase access. Already, local public libraries are helping their communities by providing multiple services and programs to library patrons. For example, the Toronto Public Library has a service whereby people can borrow a laptop for use in the library. Beyond this, there is the Computer Learning Centre, where people can learn the basics of using a computer and the Internet; and the Digital Innovation Hub, where people can learn such advanced computer skills as 3D printing and design, Web design, audio/video production, and photography.

The Toronto Public Library is far from alone in its endeavors to improve community access to the digital world — the Calgary Public Library does the same. Along with hosting publicly accessible computers and Wi-Fi Internet access, the Calgary Public Library offers a Learning Lab, where two or three technology- and software-related classes are held daily. Among its many educational programs are computer-oriented programs, such as Computer Buddies, which pairs children of under six years of age with teen volunteers who teach about searching the Internet safely and use common programs such as Microsoft Word, Excel, and PowerPoint.

Aside from its province-wide Wi-Fi hot-spot network, Newfoundland & Labrador Public Libraries hosts publicly accessible computers. Library patrons have access to the Internet and most of today's common office software, as well as to document and photo scanners, and laser and color printing. Numerous educational programs are offered.

The technology is there, in the local community: school leaders just have to help make community members aware of it.

Wi-Fi Access: Library Examples

Toronto Public Library — Computers, Internet Access, & Digital Service: http://www.torontopubliclibrary. ca/using-the-library/computer-services/

Calgary Public Library — Computers & Internet Access: http://calgarypubliclibrary.com/ services/computers-internet-access

Newfoundland & Labrador Public Libraries — Computer & Internet: http://www.nlpl.ca/index.php/ services/computers-internet.html

Achieving Access Through Recycled Technology

1. Computers for Schools (CFS), an initiative of the Canadian government, works with public and private donors to recycle computers. It collects, repairs, and distributes them to schools, not-for-profit organizations, public libraries, and First Nations communities. Computers for Schools helps to lessen the digital divide by providing computer access to the public while reducing computer hardware waste. It also employs youth in the Technical Work Experience Program (TWEP) to ensure that young people receive the work experience needed to launch their careers.

http://www.ic.gc.ca/eic/site/cfs-ope.nsf/eng/home

2. Think Recycle is a fundraising program that encourages communities to donate their unwanted mobile phones, laptops, and printer cartridges. Organizations that

participate in Think Recycle include charities, such as the Canadian Diabetes Association, Goodwill, and Habitat for Humanity; schools; churches; service clubs, such as Lions Clubs International and Rotary International; Computers for Kids; and Regina Food Bank. Members are given cash rewards for their donations which can then be used for their own fundraising program. Think Recycle also plants trees to help reduce the carbon footprints.
http://www.thinkrecycle.com/en/tree-planting

3. The ERA, or Electronic Recycling Association, aims to collect and refurbish old computers, laptops, and associated equipment to donate to non-profit and charity associations, schools, daycares, and seniors' centers, especially in Calgary, Edmonton, and Vancouver. It strives to reduce electronic waste while providing the non-profit sector with digital access.
http://www.era.ca/

4. Many computers and related pieces of equipment (e.g., ink cartridges, monitors, and printers) are regularly discarded in landfills across North America. This equipment, however, may have several years of practical functions remaining and is sometimes donated to non-profit organizations. Your school may be able to gain access to some through technology recycling websites, such as Share the Technology Computer Recycling Project. This project assists potential donors in locating a non-profit organization in the area that accepts donations through searching their computer database.
http://www.envirolink.org/resource.html?itemid=200211211049020.236091&catid=5

5. To encourage the recycling of used computer equipment, the U.S. General Services Administration has officially sponsored the Computers for Learning (CFL) program. The CFL program facilitates government donations of surplus computers. Eligible recipients may visit the CFL website to view the available computer equipment that participating government agencies have reported as surplus.
http://computersforlearning.gov/

6. Project Tomorrow, in operation for about 20 years, is a U.S. non-profit education organization with the mission "Preparing today's students to be tomorrow's innovators, leaders and engaged citizens." Its website offers a variety of programs for administrators and students.
http://www.tomorrow.org/

7. The Digital Wish Foundation is a non-profit organization designed to close digital technology gaps in the U.S. school system. Teachers, supporters, and parent–teacher groups may visit the website to view online tools and promotions, updated daily. The website also allows a wish list to be made so that community members can visit the site to become aware of classroom needs. Making a wish list with the foundation registers applicants for certain eligible matching grants. Fundraisers and recycling drives may also be organized through the site. Since 2009, the foundation has delivered more than $10 million in technology products and granted more than 24 000 wishes related to technology.
http://www.digitalwish.com/dw/digitalwish/home

Setting appropriate limits to digital access in school

Methods of communication have evolved in the digital universe to include email, instant messaging, blogging, social networking (with sites such as Facebook, MSN, Twitter, Tumblr, and Pinterest), online gaming communities (Xbox Live, PlayStation Network), and cellphone communication, such as texting and video conferencing. In addition, most smartphones and iPads are equipped with cameras with a range of websites catering to photo-sharing communities (e.g., social networks, Instagram, and Flickr). The school community needs to address the matter of appropriate methods of communication, that is to say, *socially responsible* methods — nondisruptive, time efficient, and risk free.

In particular, the digital principal is called to address the following issues through education about school policies pertaining to digital use:

- how and when students can use cellphones during school hours
- email confidentiality and safety concerns, which may include the potential for communication to be received by those not the intended recipients
- the appropriate use of photos and cameras during school hours or on school property

The choice to utilize digital devices in schools must be based carefully on their educational value and supported by existing policy and research.

Ribble and Bailey (2007) would expect the digital principal to attend to the following four questions: "How do these communication methods fit in an educational setting? What positive outcomes do they enable? What potentially negative effects must be mitigated, and how? If these technologies are banned in schools, what message does that send to our students who have access to these devices outside of school?" (p. 19). A frame based on these questions is provided in the margin. Note, though, the idea of one educator acting as the sole arbiter of digital education policy is obsolete and may be a detriment to digital education policy and practice.

Providing Guidance on Legal Use of Technology

Responsible digital citizenship warrants that the digital principal will emphasize policies, guidelines, and ethical behavior to ensure safe and legal online activity for the school community. Issues pertaining to online activity include pirating, unauthorized file-sharing, subverting Digital Rights Management (DRM) technologies, hacking into systems or networks, plagiarizing through use of online technologies, cyberbullying, committing identity theft, phishing, online stalking, distributing viruses, and encountering or making terrorist or violent threats. Under the digital principal, the school educates the community about the adverse effects of using digital technologies irresponsibly. This type of education prepares students to understand the implications of their actions and digital choices.

"Laws related to technology use are becoming more of an issue for school districts," report Ribble and Bailey (2007). "Administrators need to provide teachers and students with resources and guidance on what is legal and illegal; they also need to determine whether their technology rules and policies are supported legally" (p. 27).

Communication Method:

How does this fit in an educational setting?
What positive outcomes might this enable?
What negative effects might there be?
How can these effects be mitigated?
Should we ban this technology from school?
If we did, what would students who have access to it understand by this?

Digital Rights Management technologies are technologies developed by manufacturers, publishers, and other individuals to control how technology and its content is used.

Phishing is an attempt to gain access to personal information usually through a fraudulent email.

Presenting clear and concise rules on appropriate online activity will empower staff and students through knowledge of copyrighted versus public domain items, free versus paid items, and legal versus illegal sharing of appropriate items online. In determining legal use of technology in your school, consider:

- Are we using the technology the way we are supposed to use it?
- Are we using it responsibly?

Both users and policy makers should keep these questions in mind.

An Acceptable Use Policy Unique to Each School

Your district school board is certain to have a strategic technology plan already in place. In most cases, such a plan comes with policies and procedures intended to make implementation of technology innovation run smoothly; however, your school needs more than that. In addition to policies on purchasing new technologies, maintaining teacher professional development, and ensuring equitable access, each school requires its own Acceptable Use Policy, which will outline expectations for students using the technology. This policy, or set of procedures, should clearly define how, when, and where the computer technology may be used, and how students can protect their personal safety and privacy. An effective policy also addresses the kinds of activities that are unacceptable: these will include plagiarism and infringement of copyright. It clearly outlines disciplinary consequences for any students (and staff) who violate the policy. It is founded on the premise that everyone is expected to make responsible choices.

Sample Acceptable Use Policy
Use of the Technology
- Use computing technology as instructed or approved.
- Follow the school guidelines when using and downloading any files and software.
- Report all instances of hardware damage or changes to the desktop or operating system immediately.
- Use only authorized equipment, software, and media files, such as games.
- Do not install, access, or share anything that does not meet this criterion.
- Use the technology only for school purposes — do not buy or sell anything through school equipment.

Use of Web Content — Copyright and Permission
- Cite information from the Internet accurately, and obtain permission for use for any materials subject to copyright.
- The school abides by copyright laws. That means downloading and sharing copyrighted materials without the copyright holder's permission is not permitted.
- Plagiarism, or the act of taking another's thoughts, words, or writings as one's own, will not be tolerated.
- Visit only acceptable sites and engage in only legal online activity. If in any doubt about what is an acceptable site or an appropriate online activity, consult your teacher. Any visits outside the limits will lead to disciplinary action.

Protection and Security

- If you experience any bullying or threatening behavior online, report it to your teacher or the principal as soon as possible.
- Bullying or threatening behavior, such as cyberbullying, making online threats, or posting inappropriate material to a social media site, will not be tolerated.
- Be careful to keep passwords and data private, and do not misrepresent your identity.

The Consortium for School Networking (CoSN) website identifies five elements to consider when designing an Acceptable Use Policy for a school:

1. Access by minors to inappropriate matter on the Internet;
2. The safety and security of minors when using electronic mail, chat rooms and other forms of direct electronic communications;
3. Unauthorized access, including so-called "hacking," and other unlawful activities by minors online;
4. Unauthorized disclosure, use, and dissemination of personal information regarding minors; and
5. Measures restricting minors' access to materials harmful to them.

Essentially, a successful Acceptable Use Policy for online activity grows out of a joint effort by the principal, staff, and school community. It focuses on how to protect children and adolescents from accessing inappropriate or dangerous content and communications; it limits unauthorized access and exchange of personal information online, both outside school and at school. Further, it addresses appropriate online behavior towards others, respect for their privacy and their time, and respect for others' online property or intellectual property; it would also discourage plagiarism and abuse, and encourage critical thinking and citizenship education. Collaborative discussions with teachers, students, and parents will ensure implementation.

It is essential to provide professional development for teachers to become familiar with the Acceptable Use Policy and to clarify their understanding of it. Displaying the AUP policy in the school and sending parents copies will aid in getting everyone to assume personal ownership and responsibility.

Considering acceptable use of students' personal devices

Many students have personal devices, such as smartphones and iPods. How might an Acceptable Use Policy address their use of these portable devices? *Should* personal devices be considered? What complications could arise from limiting access on these devices in areas that are equipped with mobile network connectivity?

There is much uncertainty about the role of these devices in schools. For example, some schools have open policy on the use of cellphones and ask that students learn proper protocols and etiquette for their use. If a student is found misusing the phone, it is confiscated and held in the main office until the student speaks with an administrator to have the phone returned. In more serious cases, where bullying or repeated and serious misuse of the phone has occurred, the administrator asks for a parent to retrieve the phone, and the student is no longer permitted to use it on school property.

We observe that an increasing number of school policies limit cellphone use in the classroom, in part, to avoid potentially dangerous or inappropriate technology use in school; however, as more schools see the benefits of using such mobile technologies for teaching and engaging students, and the Bring Your Own Device trend grows, these policies will have to be revised accordingly.

We suggest that students be permitted to use personal electronic devices (PEDs) in school under conditions such as the following. Students can connect to the school network for Internet access only; unless the teacher has granted permission, they cannot use their devices in examination rooms. Students may not install any Board-licensed software, unless the software has been licensed for home use. Board technical support will not be provided for any hardware, software, or connectivity issues with personal electronic devices. Students cannot take pictures or capture video with their devices in private areas such as washrooms and change rooms. Any pictures or videos taken on school property or at a school event may be published electronically only with the permission of the individual, a parent of the student, and/or the principal.

A description of safe, acceptable use of digital technologies might be as follows: that students will not post personal information about themselves or others, including full name, age, sex, home address, telephone numbers, pictures, videos, routes taken to school, and parents' hours of work; that they will inform the teacher immediately when accidental access to inappropriate materials or contact with unacceptable users has been made; and that they will seek help from principals, teachers, and parents when victimized by cyberbullying. Students are expected to report any cyberbullying they experience or witness to principals, teachers, and parents (see Cyberbullying and How to Address It in School, below).

Further ways to promote personal responsibility

Implementing a citizenship contract school-wide and offering a digital citizenship boot camp are two ways of reinforcing the values of a school's Acceptable Use Policy.

Digital citizenship contract: Promote personal digital responsibility in your school by annually having each student sign a copy of a Citizenship Contract, a document centered on a set of about 10 principles, such as having respect for yourself and others. School assemblies are a wonderful way for the school community to review such a contract. They also provide an opportunity for students to discuss their thoughts and concerns as a student body.

You can make further connection to your school community by sending home to parents a copy of the school's digital citizenship contract or posting the contract on the school website. Hosting a parent session is also a good idea. If you explain how the school is working with students to promote digital responsibility through such a contract, parents will understand the school's approach to acting responsibly in a digital environment. At some schools, parents are asked to sign a contract of what they undertake to do with their children to promote responsible citizenship.

The Calgary Board of Education has provided an interesting model with their "Digital Citizenship at Evergreen School." This initiative seeks to engage the school board, teachers, students, and parents in a contract that facilitates the development of students into digital citizens who are respectful and responsible to others. Setting a personal contract in motion with students compels them to

---

"We share relevant literature through staff memos and during staff meetings. Our school safe-and-caring-school focus was online respect and safety. We did a poster campaign dealing with sharing info online."

— Principal Ian Wyatt

Sample Contract Principle

I will remember to balance my use of technology with other activities.

Citizenship Contract Models

See the Digital Citizenship website for pdf samples of child and parent pledges pertaining to digital citizenship:
http://www.digitalcitizenship.net.
See the Calgary model of a citizenship contract:
http://schools.cbe.ab.ca/b401/digcitevergreen.htm.

think about their actions online and the negative consequences they would face should they conduct inappropriate online activity. Engaging parents in the process of citizenship contracting allows for the fostering of an important partnership between school and home; it also expands the realm of responsible global citizenship beyond the school practices of students.

Digital citizenship boot camp: Students in some school districts are required to attend a digital citizenship boot camp in order to be able to use the wireless Internet on their mobile devices at school.

An example of a digital boot camp is St. Gregory's Grade 6 digital boot camp, as held in 2011. On the first day, students created their own definition of digital citizenship (in groups), learned about Respect, Education, and Protection of the digital self (REPs), and performed a digital distraction activity involving simultaneously writing an email and a spelling test. The second day, students watched videos and discussed appropriate device use and Internet safety, especially in relation to social networking sites (SNS). On the final day, they learned about cyberbullying and respectful digital use: participants discussed the "what, so what, and now what" of various scenarios and applied their knowledge to their own lives, such as the rules on SNS websites and at school.

The value of such personal responsibility training for online activity is evident in students' use of critical thinking, in its citizenship education dimension, and in its role in lessening the digital divide in a regulated and secure setting.

How to Help Parents Reinforce Safe Digital Practices

As a prudent administrator, the digital principal will enlist parents and guardians in promoting safe digital practices. Providing literature from the school about safe and educational online practices invites parents to be a part of the learning process. Regular communication between parents and teachers about online activities at home and in the school is necessary. The digital principal promotes this kind of communication to ensure that the monitoring of online behaviors is appropriate and informed.

Effective schools help parents find ways to engage in conversations about online activities. Trying to speak to children about their online activities is a challenge for many parents. Parents may not be fully up-to-date on social networking terminology or understand how social media are an integral part of their children's lives. The natural developmental phase of adolescents seeking more independence further complicates efforts to talk about online activities.

Below are several concrete pieces of advice that could be shared with parents and guardians of students.

How to Help Young People Develop Online Limits

- Build a relationship of trust with your child online. Explain that the Internet is not a private place and that everyone can look at what the child is doing.
- Identify safety as the first concern, not the last.
- Encourage your child to trust his or her instincts. If something does not feel right and seems to present danger, then the child should tell you or another trusted adult.
- Explain that people often lie on the Internet, and just as your child may have an avatar, or a re-creation of the ideal self, adults can pretend that they are children or children can pose as adults.

- Bring to your child's attention that videos, pictures, and anything else posted on the Internet can live forever, so thinking twice about what is posted is important.
- Explain that your child may find content that is not appropriate because the Internet is uncensored. Encourage your child to report anything inappropriate; strive to ensure that your search engines are child safe.
- Set rules! Make sure that your child understands what is appropriate and what is not. Require that friends who visit follow the same protocols.

The digital principal actively involves parents in a coordinated effort to regulate student online practices. Doing so requires speaking to the children about acceptable and safe use of digital technology in a consistent way, and school and parents setting similar expectations for ethical behavior online. Common reinforcement at school and at home will help to equip students with digital citizenship skills. For example, both school and home may view time on social media sites such as Facebook and Twitter as distractions and so discourage going there; and both may monitor children's computer use during schoolwork.

The digital principal reaches out to parents to provide education and support with regard to technology. Information on the latest technologies and safe online behavior can be communicated through parent newsletters, parent–teacher nights, and the school website. Other forums are technology workshops, tutorials, and courses at school or a nearby university. Topics may include online privacy, online safety, and how to properly use social media networking sites, such as Facebook and Twitter. Administrators need to consider who will be responsible for organizing and educating parents in these initiatives, and where this information can be obtained.

Administrators can help foster a home climate in which parents are well positioned to promote healthy online activity for their child. Elementary vice-principal Joanne Anthony, for example, has encouraged parents to understand digital citizenship through making a virtual family visit to many of the student website links on the school site — many sites can make learning engaging and fun while building particular literacy skills. She also promotes Brainpop.com within her school community because having families invest time in collaborative learning strengthens the bond of the family learning relationship at home. She points out that parents' digital involvement in their child's learning invites them to see how their child's skills in digital literacies are developing in tandem with valuable school skills. This type of engagement can open up the conversation on online activities and how to negotiate them.

In part as a result of school outreach, parents can take measures to ensure the safety of their children's online activities. They can monitor online activity by putting the computer in a common area of the home, where it would be easy for them to keep an eye on their children. They can create rules with their children — perhaps no video-game or computer time until homework is finished. They can also gain exposure to the digital media their children are using and thereby learn more about the appropriateness of their media use (perhaps adding a child as a friend on Facebook, if they are regular users, or sending texts, if they frequently text). Further, they can talk with their children about safe media and social media network use.

Although we consider it desirable for parents to be in constant dialogue with their children about issues of privacy, we know that this is not always possible. We recommend that parents have an understanding with each child of how and

For helpful ideas on facilitating children's safe use of online resources, check out "Internet Safety Tips for Parents," a two-page document prepared by the British Columbia Ministry of Education: http://www.bced.gov.bc.ca/sco/resourcedocs/internet_safe/internet_safe.pdf.

when the parents can enter into the child's private cyberspace. For example, some parents have friended their children on Facebook and check text-messaging on their mobile devices regularly. Having direct conversation while navigating school-related websites, such as www.brainpop.com, or YouTube, or helping a child with online research may allow parents to introduce critical online skills.

Setting parameters for children's online activity

The following ideas are meant to be shared with parents.

- Discuss what the child can access online, perhaps websites, chat rooms, and gaming communities. With the child, visit the sites in question. Explore each one. Discuss safe use and interactions. Your monitoring and filtering will work better than setting up any formal filtering options such as Safe-Search on YouTube. The goal is to help children understand how to stay safe.
- Discuss with the child how privacy is enacted in your home. What are some rules? Explain how privacy is not always adhered to in cyberspace. In other words, your child should not put anything out there unless prepared for everyone to read or see it. Look on the Internet together, visiting different chat forums and YouTube channels, and talk about what public versus private communication entails.
- Show consistency in your approach and rules. You may want to develop a family agreement outlining time that can be spent online, sites the child may visit, and expected behavior. Ensure that you have established boundaries. Assure your child that he or she can talk about issues without necessarily getting into trouble.
- Ensure that the child knows how to make immediate choices to avoid content or contact in a situation of potential danger. Show how to turn off the screen, exit the website, or turn off the iPad or phone.
- Be mindful of how easy it is for younger children to navigate themselves into dangerous areas unintentionally. Set up bookmarks to help your child find the content desired.

The importance of monitoring students' use of digital spaces

School administrators and parents are wise to acquaint themselves with content-blocking programs that can restrict the types of information that students and children can access on school and home computers. Institution of such programs will avoid some of the worries associated with children's online activity.

Education is the best way to protect children from online predators, who often access and create account profiles on websites frequented by children. These include virtual worlds and chat rooms. Predators regularly pose as children themselves.

Encourage parents to be mindful of the dangers posed to young children and to monitor their children's interactions in virtual space. Encourage both parents and teachers to talk to children about sexual predators and potential online dangers. As for really young children, reinforce the idea that they should not use chat rooms unless online moderators and parental supervision are present — the dangers are too great.

Questions for Parents to Consider
- Do you intend to review your child's online messages?
- At what point are the messages no longer private?
- How often do you expect to view your child's messages?

Promoting Responsible Sharing Online

"We let the students know how important it is to be responsible online. Through the use of an extensive and ongoing poster campaign (via the Kids Help Phone network) and guest speakers, we keep the issue in rotation. This upcoming year will focus on the implications of "sexting" and how your private info should be shared responsibly."

— Principal Ian Davidson

As part of your digital outreach to parents, convey to them and their children the importance of monitoring the digital spaces that children frequent online. As children get older, suggest that they be directed towards well-monitored children's chat rooms; encourage teenagers to use monitored chat rooms, too, keeping to the public area. Make parents and staff aware that many chat rooms offer private areas where users can have one-on-one chats with other users: children should avoid these "whisper" areas because chat monitors cannot read these private conversations. Help children and their parents understand that they are not to respond to instant messages or emails from strangers; encourage them to notify the teacher or you as the principal right away. Where there has been contact with a person not known to the child or the supervising adult, it may be a good idea to make a report to the school board and police department.

Awareness raising on risks associated with online activity

All school community members need to be familiar with the potential dangers of online activities. You can share the information in a list, such as that beginning on page 116, on your school website or blog, or present it in your school e-newsletter. "Potential Dangers of Online Activities" is directed to parents and guardians, and can be adapted to suit the age range of the students. Encourage educators to discuss its content in class lessons, reaching educational outcomes while informing on safe educational practices (e.g., create a Venn diagram in math or science, focused on what bullying and cyberbullying have and do not have in common; or make a summary of the e-newsletter article in language arts). Administrators need to promote safe practices through school-wide programs or campaigns such as a poster competition or other initiative that raises awareness.

Promoting Responsible Social Interactions

With digital technology use come responsibilities. "As members of a digital society, we are asked to do what is best for the larger group," write Ribble and Bailey (2007). "To do this, we must think about how our technology use affects others. Good digital citizens respect others and learn ways to use technology courteously and effectively" (p. 25). Part of our role is to ensure that students are using technology the way it is intended and hence, not infringing upon the rights of others.

How can students — and staff — be accountable for using digital technologies? Ribble and Bailey (2007) provide an answer, in two parts: (1) "Following acceptable user policies and using technology responsibly both inside and outside school, using online material ethically, including citing sources and requesting permissions, reporting cyberbullies, threats, and other inappropriate use" (p. 30); and (2) protecting hardware and network security; protecting personal security (dangers: identity theft, phishing, and online stalking); protecting school security (dangers: hackers and viruses); and finally, protecting community security (danger: terrorist threats) (p. 34).

Here, we focus on the first part, going beyond policy to behavior. The digital principal needs to discuss with students and staff members the issue of plagiarism and the penalties associated with it, copyright law and its infringement, cyberbullying and how to address it, and the need for netiquette. The digital principal will promote and model appropriate social interactions.

Potential Dangers of Online Activities

Different online activities may pose different risks to your children, although many overlap considerably. Here, we will outline the risks associated with a variety of online environments and offer ideas on how to lower them.

Online Gaming Online games come with risks that include sexually explicit or obscene language in chats, exposure to sexually explicit or obscene avatars created by other players, receiving of website links leading to inappropriate content, and certain games having available downloads ("mods") that could contain viruses or malware. With online gaming, there also is a risk that children could unknowingly come in contact with sexual predators.

What to do: Advise children to stay safe by not communicating with strangers and never giving out personal information or photos to other players in the game. Encourage game play with a parent present or on sites with moderators who check the players' behavior. Monitors send email notifications to parents when children do not play the game by the established rules or when bullying occurs.

Search Engines Use of search engines can lead children to sexually explicit, violent, or otherwise inappropriate material. Children may inadvertently increase this risk by using incorrect spelling in searches and address bars, and using improper search techniques.

What to do: Using search engines such as Google's SafeSearch will ensure that searching the Internet will always be safe, with inappropriate content blocked.

Social Networking Websites These websites have many of the same dangers of real-world interaction, and when these dangers are combined with online dangers, it becomes particularly important that children know about online safety. Social networking websites are often prone to cyberbullying. Children could be connecting with people they do not know — it is often difficult to verify the true identity of an account holder. Many sexual predators use social networking to engage children. *Sexting*, or the posting and sharing of sexually explicit adult content, has been a problem in some intermediate and senior schools. In some cases, children have taken pictures of themselves and others in sexual activities, which can be hosted on websites ascribing to this sexual content. Mobile devices offer easy ways for content to be placed online.

What to do: Children need to know that they should never accept a friend request from someone they have not met and that they should be careful what they send to whom online. Once a message, photo, or video is sent, it is no longer controlled by the sender — it can be forwarded or reproduced without permission. As for sexting, with its misuse of mobile phone cameras, help children to understand how the practice is dangerous and illegal, and has long-term consequences for all involved.

Instant Messaging and Email The risks of instant messaging and email typically come from unknown links or downloads that children may click on. These links or downloads may expose your computer to viruses or malware, or could lead your children to inappropriate content.

Pembroke Publishers ©2014 *The Digital Principal* by Janette Hughes, Anne Burke ISBN 9781-55138-288-3

Information sent over instant messaging or emails cannot be unsent. Users need to be aware that digital communication is permanent and can be saved and shared with others.

What to do: Tell children about the permanent nature of digital communication, and promote safe practices such as reviewing emails before sending them and thinking about what could happen if the messages are shared with others.

Cellphones and Texting Some cellphones have Internet access, through which children can be exposed to violent, sexual, or inappropriate content. Cellphones are also susceptible to malware and viruses. Clicking on unknown links increases this risk. Other considerations: Photos and videos taken from cellphones can disclose location, children can be photographed or recorded without their knowledge, and using GPS, children can be tracked by the locations of their phones. Cellphones and texting can also make children more accessible to cyberbullies and sexual predators.

What to do: Tell children not to share personal information or photos via their cellphones and to be careful what they download on cellphones — apps, games, ringtones — because these could contain viruses, malware (from the words *malicious* and *software*), or hidden fees. Teach children safety-conscious digital skills, such as creating user names that do not reveal name or gender. Actively consider and perhaps reassess whether children are old enough and mature enough to use cellphones in a responsible way.

Chat Rooms Chat rooms pose risks because children can be exposed to cyberbullies, viruses, malware, and inappropriate, violent, or sexual content.

What to do: Tell children not to send any personal information or photos, to talk only to people they know in person, and not to click on any unknown links.

Peer-to-Peer File Sharing Children can be exposed to inappropriate content; filenames can be changed and may not necessarily reflect file content. Downloads can also come with viruses or malware.

What to do: Tell children to use reliable websites and to turn on virus protection software to scan any and all downloads from the Internet. Administrators and parents can minimize the risk of viruses by providing virus protection and firewalls on all computers.

Video-Sharing Websites Video-sharing websites run the risk of exposing children to sexually explicit, violent, or otherwise inappropriate content. Sexual predators may use these websites to coerce children into posting or sending videos of themselves.

What to do: Remind children not to give out personal information and to avoid clicking on unknown links or requests.

Webcams These can be dangerous for children because once the videos are sent, they are no longer controlled by the sender. Sexual predators may also be able to coerce children into using a webcam or may see previously posted images to threaten or harass a child.

What to do: Have open communication with children about mean or threatening behavior online. Encourage them to talk about any bullying or harassment that happens there.

Pembroke Publishers ©2014 *The Digital Principal* by Janette Hughes, Anne Burke ISBN 9781-55138-288-3

Plagiarism and How to Help Students Avoid It

Plagiarism involves the misappropriation of intellectual sources, and false representation of "original work." It is an act of fraud and is a serious ethical offence in the academic community. It involves not only stealing someone else's work, but lying about it, as well. Intellectual property is protected by copyright laws, and is defined as "creations of the mind, such as inventions; literary and artistic works, designs; and symbols, names and images used in commerce" (www.wipo. int/about-ip/en/).

Plagiarism may include, but is not limited to

- using someone else's work as your own
- using someone else's words or ideas, uncredited
- failing to properly quote sources
- using incorrect citation information

Plagiarism is not always a black-and-white issue. There are many different types, some pertaining to the proper citation of source and reference material. When confronted with possible cases of academic dishonesty, consider these two scenarios and the range of behaviors they represent.

1. Sources not cited

The writer turns in another author's work as his or her own.

The writer copies large portions of a work, without paraphrasing or identifying the source.

The writer sews together work from several sources.

The writer keeps the general ideas and content of another source, but changes key words.

The writer paraphrases other sources in place of original work.

The writer uses his or her own previous work, passing it off as new.

2. Sources cited

Mention of source's name is given, but details of the source are omitted.

The writer incorrectly cites sources, making them difficult or impossible to trace.

The writer neglects to use quotation properly.

The paper is properly cited but contains no original work.

The writer properly cites some sources but neglects to cite paraphrased material.

It is important for administrators and teachers to instil in students a sense of *academic integrity*. Students need to understand this concept, and doing so begins with understanding what plagiarism is, what counts as plagiarism, and what the consequences of plagiarism are. To start, teachers must be familiar with their school board's policy on plagiarism. You have a role to play in ensuring that they are.

Consider why a student might plagiarize. The reasons will vary from student to student, but may include a misunderstanding of the assignment or material, or ignorance. Students may demonstrate carelessness or take notes poorly. Stress and competition among students is another important factor to consider. Students may have poor time management skills and not be able to plan effectively for successful completion of an assignment. Lack of individual confidence or the perceived cheating of others may lead to student plagiarism. Further, low-level assignments that do not stimulate critical thinking may be prone to plagiarism. Finally, assessments that emphasize the product, with little or no consideration of the process, may lead students to plagiarize their submission material.

Avoiding conditions that promote plagiarism

The positive side of these issues is that they can all be addressed by teachers and administrators. Administrators can keep to developed policies and protocols to help teachers, the student body, and parents in having a clear understanding of the consequences of plagiarism. A focused-on-learning approach would be epitomized by an administrator advocating for assessment that follows a process route whereby work is submitted in stages.

Teachers can help avoid plagiarism by the way they structure their projects: they can assign specific topics or questions and then ask that students submit their work in stages or as a process of several writing drafts. For example, each student could submit a thesis statement, followed by an outline, a first draft, and so on. Teachers could ask students to annotate their bibliographies to demonstrate a certain level of familiarity with the source material for their assignment. They may assign oral presentations to their students or require that sources used for an assignment be recent publications that are printed out and submitted with the final assignment. Teachers may also request that each student submit a paragraph on the composition process so that they can gain a sense of the student's writing ability. Beyond that, effective teachers will encourage students to write concisely, a practice that calls upon writers to put text in their own words. In any event, they are responsible for ensuring that students clearly understand what is expected of them.

As a digital principal, you will want to ensure that you are up-to-date on several guidelines related to preventing plagiarism and that you review these guidelines with staff. One approach is to directly explain to teachers what plagiarism is and why it is wrong. Stress to teachers that the best way to prevent plagiarism is by teaching information literacy skills, such as paraphrasing, documentation, and citation, to help students properly use sources when researching and writing. Teaching time management, as well as building time into the schedule for work on assignments, will model for students how to use writing process time effectively; it will also show an appreciation of how students may become overwhelmed by course work if these skills are not used. Finally, providing frequent feedback and encouragement, and, as noted above, designing assignments in stages to assess both process and result can help students develop honest writing practices.

For any student who does submit plagiarized work, there need to be consequences clearly and explicitly outlined and enforced. For example, teachers may require that the student redo the assignment, submit supplementary work showing that he or she understands the assignment, or assign a grade penalty. According to the Halton District School Board policy on cheating and plagiarism, administrators may limit a student's participation in school activities or eligibility for awards, meet with the student's parents or guardians, or suspend the student (see http://www.hdsb.ca/Policy/Cheating%20Plagarism.pdf).

Policies pertaining to plagiarism vary according to the school and school board policy; all educators should be familiar with their employer's policies.

Copyright Concerns as a Digital Citizenship Issue

Teachers rely on many different resources in the 21st century classroom. They have been able to move beyond textbooks and lectures. Now, they can use videos, games, music, and the Internet to embellish their lessons. Many of these resources are subject to copyright laws, and educators need to know how to use the resources to advantage in a way that does not violate the law.

Simply put, copyright laws exist to protect the rights of creators. "Creators of original works are entitled to reasonable reward for the use of their works and protection from misuse and/or pirating of their works" (Canadian Teachers' Federation [CTF], 2011, p. 1). However, not all use of works requires permission from the creator or creators. Current copyright law in North America states that it is not an infringement to "deal fairly" with a work that is protected by copyright. The Canadian term *fair dealing* is defined by five categories of use: (1) research, (2) private study, (3) criticism, (4) review, and (5) news reporting. In the United States, the policy of "fair use" is more open-ended: it refers to limited use of copyrighted material without having to acquire permission from the rights holder for educational and other purposes. All administrators, teachers, and students need to be aware of copyright laws in their own jurisdictions. It is also a good idea to be familiar with Creative Commons, a non-profit organization committed to providing and expanding works that can be used copyright free.

How do copyright laws affect teachers and students?

For further discussion and clarification, we recommend the 2012 CTF publication *Copyright Matters!* It can be found online at http://www.cmec.ca/copyrightinfo.

In Canada, there have been recent efforts to amend copyright laws, one major concern being educational distribution. The first initiative, Bill C-32, was well supported by teachers, who found two sections of the bill of particular importance for education. The Canadian Teachers' Federation approved of the move to give teachers and students free access to Internet content for educational purposes. It also agreed with the proposal that fair dealing extend to education.

Bill C-32 was succeeded by Bill C-11, which had many similar educational concerns. Passage of this bill into law as *The Copyright Modernization Act* has resulted in notable reforms, such as these:

1. *Fair dealing* was expanded to include education, as well as parody and satire.
2. *Safe harbor* is available for creators of non-commercial, user-generated content: Teachers can use this provision to create non-commercial materials.
3. The Act distinguishes between commercial and non-commercial use for the purpose of damages, something that applies to educational institutions and significantly reduces their potential liability.
4. There is a distance learning provision for online course materials, something relevant to schools in more remote areas, such as Northern Ontario.
5. There is an exception for publicly available materials on the Internet.
6. A technology-neutral provision for the reproduction of materials for display purposes, regardless of medium, opens up display permissions to the online learning context. Previously, they were only manual and via projector.
7. A provision applies to digital transmission of materials on an inter-library basis: It will increase access to information held by libraries.
8. A copyright exception for public performance in schools will reduce the licensing costs for educational institutions.

Although access to creative work is opening up for educators, there remains much to consider when learning about copyright. Administrators and teachers can lead the way in respecting copyright laws through effective modeling in practice for students. This effort will affect a variety of educational situations, ranging from what we choose to photocopy for students to the unrestricted use of video in the classroom. Modeling ethical practice is as important as teaching this knowledge to students and sharing with them the numerous resources available for their own clarification of copyright matters.

Cyberbullying and How to Address It in School

At first, the concept of "cyberbullying" may seem straightforward. We all know what bullying is, so it makes sense that, in our digital age, we could extend its definition to include digital instances of bullying. To start, the Canada Safety Council defines cyberbullying as "harmful actions that are communicated via electronic media and are intended to embarrass, harm or slander another individual" (Canada Safety Council, 2012). Similarly, *cyber bystander behaviors* are recognized as "behaviours such as passively watching someone being cyber bullied or assisting the person cyber bullying (e.g. adding more mean comments to a mean post)" (*Cyberbullying*, 2012).

Just like the technologies that support it, cyberbullying is a relatively recent phenomenon. Because of this, the legal system is still catching up with the technologies. Laws concerning cyberbullying are difficult to make and even more difficult to enforce, especially when children are involved. In Canada, efforts at legislation have been at the provincial level and subject to much criticism. For example, Nova Scotia passed a law that aims to protect victims and hold perpetrators — and their parents, in some cases — responsible for the emotional, mental, physical, and other damages that may be caused by cyberbullying (Davison, 2013); on the other hand, Quebec and Ontario have approached the problem by requiring schools to develop plans to address cyberbullying. Beyond that, the Standing Senate Committee on Human Rights is conducting an inquiry into the issue.

Cyberbullying falls into a rather grey legal area. The differences in approaches taken by the provinces mentioned may offer insight into why this may be the case. One large issue with cyberbullying is assigning responsibility. No one is quite sure whom to blame. Do we hold children responsible? How much blame can truly be placed on a child? Do we then move to blame the parents or teachers for not monitoring the children enough, or failing to teach them right from wrong? Or, do we blame corporations, such as Internet service providers, that make these communications possible?

This section will highlight some of these issues and indicate just how complicated it is to answer the question of responsibility. When the school administration encounters cyberbullying, however, the assigning of responsibility is important in determining how to proceed. As a digital principal, you will find that keeping abreast of changes in the legal ramifications of cyberbullying will aid you in efforts to have a strong community voice to address any bullying.

Children: The legislation in Nova Scotia tries to place blame, at least in part, on the children. This position is not uncommon, as both society and the legal system naturally assign blame to perpetrators; however, the position does have its critics.

Legal and social welfare experts doubt it will have much effect on behavior unless some sort of educational reform is coupled with it.

Some people question whether a purely punishment-based initiative will work in the case of cyberbullying. As Nova Scotia Justice Minister Ross Landry put it: ". . . before we vilify the cyberbullies, I think we need to recognize that a good number of the cyberbullies are really children or young people themselves, and that when they carry out this kind of behaviour in many instances they don't understand the impact of what they are doing" (Davison, 2013). This insight can prompt the digital principal to provide a clear definition of cyberbullying with examples of such behaviors. Doing so will help students and the community understand the impact of such behavior and how it affects everyone.

Internet Service Providers (ISPs): Some have questioned the Internet service providers' role in cyberbullying, but it is not always possible to show any knowledge of the activity on the part of service providers. Like cellphone companies, they are often mere conduits for information.

Parents: Nova Scotia's new legislation allows for parents to be held legally responsible in cases of cyberbullying. This approach has been heavily criticized for many reasons. It is difficult to hold parents responsible for everything their child does, especially when it is online and may easily go unnoticed. While holding parents responsible may be effective in some cases of negligence, the greater objective needs to be educating the parents, helping them to understand the problem and providing support.

School Administrators and Teachers: Principals and teachers are often uncertain as to where their responsibilities as supervisors and caregivers lie, as well as what the boundaries of their roles are. Yet much of the online activity and cyberbullying take place during the school day. Many ask to what extent schools are responsible for the digital activity that takes place during this time.

The need for a cooperative effort

Several factors, most notably the involvement of children, make cyberbullying especially difficult to address. Because of this, assigning sole responsibility is nearly impossible. What, then, can be done about cyberbullying? Any and all action will require a cooperative effort.

"It requires a sense of collective responsibility that all of us as responsible citizens can do something to take steps to address the problem of cyberbullying," says Marvin Bernstein, UNICEF Canada's chief policy adviser (Davison, 2013). Dealing effectively with cyberbullying demands a multi-faceted approach that fosters a sense of responsibility about online behavior — and it begins with education.

The model unit plan featured as an appendix focuses on cyberbullying.

Communication between parents, teachers, and children can help the children understand what responsible online behavior looks like. The digital principal will endeavor to clearly communicate relevant school policy to all stakeholders to ensure that the legal and social repercussions of cyberbullying are understood. Effective communication will not only serve to inform children but will open up lines of communication so that young people would find it easier to tell someone about exposure to cyberbullying.

School administrators need to stay informed about the latest trends in cyberspace and how they relate to cyberbullying. Communication is the most important tool for informing school staff about current student behavior and enacting policy in regard to digital interactions in the school community. School administration is expected to promote responsible online behavior through policy and programming that target cyberbullying and its repercussions.

What to do when a student reports cyberbullying

First and foremost, principals and teachers need to be familiar with their school's policy on bullying, the use of technology, and cyberbullying more specifically, in order to respond effectively to incidents. The digital principal clearly and concisely communicates school policy and creates an atmosphere that encourages frequent discussion about the responsible use of digital devices so that teachers will have the support they need to respond in an appropriate and supportive manner.

The Canada Safety Council has outlined key steps for educators to follow when responding to incidents of cyberbullying. Part of the principal's role is to ensure that the staff is aware of their responsibilities.

1. Upon receiving a report of cyberbullying, the teacher ensures that there is no immediate risk and that the student is safe from danger. Listening to the student is important.

   Tell teachers that they should never dismiss what the student is feeling — cyberbullying must be taken as seriously as face-to-face bullying.
2. The teacher gathers any and all documentation available about the incident(s), including any reports from witnesses. It is recommended that the student who was bullied do the same, saving the online bullying communication.

   Advise teachers to be open and honest with any student in these circumstances, but not to promise secrecy. Tell them to let students know that their responsibilities as an educator may include bringing the incident of cyberbullying to your attention and that of the police.
3. Advise the teacher to meet with the bullied student's parents and to notify other teachers of the report of cyberbullying. The teacher may need to refer the student and parents to appropriate authorities (e.g., police, service providers). It is equally important for the first teacher to follow up with the student — if the student initiated contact, he or she is likely to feel comfortable continuing with that line of communication.
4. Keep in mind that prevention can be the most integral part of an educator's role in any approach to cyberbullying. Consider building class lessons about cyberbullying and online behavior. School-wide programming that focuses on character development (e.g., social justice, Lions Quest) may introduce concepts that relate to respectful and responsible digital use. Encourage teachers to strive to make their students see them as allies, as people to talk to if they have issues or questions about cyberbullying.

Netiquette

Principals may act as important models in terms of responsible social interactions that are mediated by digital technologies. They may establish policies related to the safe, ethical, and legal use of digital information and technology in the classroom, and then model these behaviors accordingly. Beyond that, they can promote the adoption of guidelines on social interactions mediated by digital technologies and model their appropriate use.

Netiquette, which can easily relate to school citizenship initiatives, is understood as the code of conduct for polite and appropriate use of the Internet. There are several measures that administrators can take to encourage students to adopt netiquette as a way to promote safe and healthy online interactions. Most obviously, there is the consideration that students be polite in online activities; beyond that, netiquette encompasses several more online behaviors that relate to safety and security issues. Students following netiquette use appropriate language (not obscene, profane, threatening, harassing, bullying, violent, homophobic, racist, sexist, and disrespectful language), whether posted publicly, privately, or on websites. They refrain from sending messages that contain information that would cause discomfort to themselves or others if written on a classroom chalkboard or appearing in another public place. They limit their use of the computing technology to ways that are conducive to the learning of their peers (in other words, ways that will not disrupt other users). They do not try to "hack" the Board network or any other computer network, nor attempt to harm or compromise the functionality of the system. With netiquette in place, students are expected to assume that all communications received are private and confidential; as a result, they will not disseminate any of them without permission from the original author. They will refrain from collecting or distributing on the Internet information that personally identifies others. Netiquette involves showing respect for others.

Administrators can provide positive reinforcement for those who promote or model respectful and responsible online practices. Ways to do so include making school-wide announcements about or conferring certificates on students who practice netiquette appropriately. Giving rewards can also encourage the continued modelling of positive behavior. Students may be granted additional access to digital technologies or time online.

In fairness to all students, the disciplinary consequences of violating official school policy are clearly outlined. There may be stipulations that the offending student will be given a notice of violation and required to meet with a school administrator. The school administrator may determine whether the violation merits the denial, restriction, or suspension of the student's access to the Board's network. If any suspicion of illegal activity arises, the administrator may consider getting in touch with the appropriate legal authorities.

Netiquette in relation to personal electronic device use

Netiquette applies to the use of personal electronic devices (PEDs) in the school. Administrators and teachers must be sure to communicate with parents or guardians about positive reinforcement for students following recommended netiquette, as well as student discipline if safe use or netiquette is ignored. It is a good idea to work with a special services team, or a team designed to meet the specific needs of students, to ensure that a holistic approach is taken to raise awareness of the importance of safe online behavior. As an administrator, you will need to ensure that students and staff are not bypassing safety and security protocols with their own devices to engage in unsafe online practices.

Student use of personal electronic devices is a privilege, not a right, so can be stopped at the principal's discretion if it interferes with student learning. We recommend that students be able to bring devices such as cellphones, tablets, and laptops to school; however, we do not recommend that students use them during class time unless given permission by the teacher. We also advise that students be responsible for securing their own devices, and for turning them off and putting them away during regular school hours unless instructed otherwise.

Beyond ensuring that all students, teachers, and staff are familiar with netiquette and aware of specific acceptable and safe use procedures, help them to understand and internalize what it means to be a good digital citizen. This knowledge will allow them to protect themselves both in and out of school. You can foster this by providing consistent messages about digital citizenship, discussed further below.

Teaching Students to Be Citizens Who Make a Difference

Digital citizenship education extends beyond the immediate school community to encompass global electronic communication and connection. In the classroom, students may be asked to make connections between various communities, perhaps urban versus rural, and draft advocacy letters to government representatives requesting more technology funding for underserved communities. In a Tech Ed classroom, students could draw on their experiences with the increase of access to networking technologies to draft a school-wide policy for fair and safe use of digital technologies. Good digital citizenship, both on local and global scales, as defined by the safe use of technologies, growth of netiquette, and critical education, could be the foundation. Students would thereby come to better understand their global and electronic reach.

Essential conditions and context

Digital citizenship is founded on three principles. First, issues of equal access must be resolved by the school administration to ensure that digital access is fair and equitable. Second, education and programming must center on the teaching of rights and responsibilities for safe use and netiquette in using online communication tools, whether for social media or video conferencing. Third, appropriate use of digital technology will encompass active citizenship training, something that involves both perception and understanding of local and global issues.

Understanding the reach of our communication channels requires us to consider the variety of platforms used in our schools. More important, we must take into account the audience that will gain access to our schools through communication platforms used as a part of everyday curricula. Work produced by students using digital technologies is not constrained by the physical classroom space: it may be disseminated at local and global levels. Approving use of personal electronic devices can extend access and mobility in school; it will also help to ensure that school community members have the tools required to be active digital citizens.

Involvement in Global Issues Through Digital Tools

"We have a very international focused school," says Principal Ian Davidson. "We have international travel clubs, Project Overseas, Global Young Leaders forum participants (both in Europe and the United States), and pen-pal projects with schools abroad. We use Skype, Edmodo, text, and email to facilitate our goals.... We strive to make our classrooms as exciting and dynamic as the world around us. To this end, an international focus is of great importance to our school and the future we strive to prepare our students for."

Civic learning

To first understand what is happening in their communities, children can engage in what is called "civic learning." Civic learning gives students a chance to talk and learn about key issues and dilemmas that arise in everyday life. It may also lead to their gaining deep understanding through conversation and inquiry-based learning. This type of learning can include mentoring arrangements, where community mentors model the roles and responsibilities of members of a civic society to their mentees, who could be students from your school. Mentors and mentees may show mutual respect while investing in the production of a valuable learning gain. Students may be encouraged to take active part in local public health projects and campaigns with mentors, perhaps helping to distribute information pamphlets at a community health fair. They may eventually choose to work in similar careers as their mentors, contributing to community life through the making of public decisions and the effecting of policies.

Civic learning helps children to understand the rights and responsibilities of citizens in a way that directly connects to their own interests, grounding their learning in meaningful practice. This sort of understanding encourages students to take responsibility for seeking solutions to civic issues, such as environmental change, immigration, and unemployment. Furthermore, civic learning encourages students to create change that will make a positive difference for others. Students become motivated to take an active and purposeful part in civic society.

A case study: Creating Glogs to promote social justice

In a classroom-based digital literacy project, we explored what happened when young adolescents were asked to engage with digital and print texts that focused on the impact of war on children. Two classes of Grade 6 students read and critiqued a variety of digital texts in literacy centers. These texts focused on the *UN Convention on the Rights of the Child* and children living in war-torn countries. In small groups, the students engaged in either literature circle or book club activities as they read young adult literature on the theme of children and war. They were then asked to conduct more research, using the computer to gather statistical and biographical data.

In the final project, students created digital and multimodal texts designed to be shared with a wider community as a way of taking action. Such projects are called "digital social justice projects." They are intended to foster the idea of equal opportunity for all society members. The digital creation of projects not only provides students with the tools and resources to find and share information, but it also helps position students as critical thinkers and users. For example, the students from one class shared the digital texts they produced at a school-wide assembly and also raised $500 to purchase chickens and a bread oven for a Third World community. Beyond that, they shared their multimodal projects in a variety of venues, including the project website, and at a classroom Ning (a social networking site set up for the project).

In this study, we found that when students were given digital tools, they embraced the ideas on digital citizenship offered by programs such as Glogster and Bitstrips. They used these programs to create digital texts intended to engage other students in discourses of social justice to inspire them to act. In this instance, we saw how the design choices for digital posters made the Glogster

Glogster for Poster Making

Glogster EDU (www.glogster.com) is the leading global educational platform. It enables students to creatively express knowledge and skills through the development of multimedia posters. It is an award-winning educational site.

site an ideal space for students to draw on their creativity and desire for digital citizenship to benefit others.

Students created interactive digital posters, or Glogs, critically combining images, texts, and sounds. The digital posters enabled the students to merge digital skills with traditional language arts learning. (They could easily use the tutorials on design offered on the Glogster site.) Students representing a variety of learning competencies found the work highly engaging.

One poster in this digital literacy center used the inspiring 2008 book *One Hen: How One Small Loan Made a Big Difference* by Katie Smith Milway. The book shows how the actions of a few can change the lives of many. *One Hen* is based on the life of Kwabena Darko, a Ghanaian whose entrepreneurial spirit grows from the loan of money to purchase a hen; Darko went on to gain a college education, run a thriving, large-scale poultry business, and give back to the community. The student who made the poster chose the book because she felt that people could be successful in their own hometowns when their opportunities are changed. In her poster, she shares: "Hard work and belief in yourself leads to success. When we have success it is important to give back to others." Her message shows her critical understanding of the power relations between and among people, and how to take action to disrupt common thinking. Demonstrating her ability to engage with the book's original design, the student adopted the illustrator's rich yellows and oranges within her own work, showing multiple visual representations of her textual response.

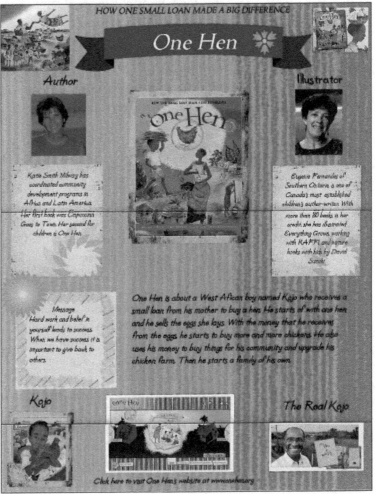

A digitally produced poster on a social justice theme

The digital literature discussions on design and poster layout that took place during the unit served to raise the students' awareness of the plight of others as presented through strategically chosen websites, novels with a social justice perspective, and picture books. Students were prompted to act. For example, their responses included hosting a school assembly, where they presented their blogs; and raising money through the school's student population for a water system.

Various digital platforms are available for educators to use as a part of the everyday curriculum. The key is using these platforms in ways that empower students to see how they can make a difference in the lives of others, as well as in their own, as contributing members of society.

Digital Platforms That Can Focus Students on Social Justice

Glogster: http://edu.glogster.com/
Bitstrips: http://www.bitstripsforschools.com/
Prezi: http://prezi.com/
Comic Master: http://www.comicmaster.org.uk/
Popplet: http://Popplet.com
My StoryMaker: http://www.clpgh.org/kids/storymaker/embed.cfm
Jux: https://jux.com/
Stixy: http://www.stixy.com/welcome
SpiderScribe: http://www.spiderscribe.net/
Storybird: http://storybird.com/
Slide.ly: http://slide.ly/

Questions to Consider:
- How can this tool be used for instruction?
- How can this tool be used to showcase a cause or take action?
- What knowledge will children gain, and how will they take agency?

Transformational Change Anchored in Digital Citizenship

Transformational leadership invites creative change in schools and communities. Strong leaders seek out such connections, aiming to make desirable changes that benefit all stakeholders. Finding diverse and innovative ways to engage students within a community, as outlined above, is transformational for all.

Because students are growing up surrounded by digital technologies, many educators think that the students already know more than they, as educators, do. Although it is true that students are often more comfortable exploring and experimenting with new technology, they may not be using it correctly or understanding its full application within the educational world. Administrators and teachers always have a valuable role to play.

We, the authors, recommend teaching students about digital citizenship and then using the initial teachings as a base for follow-up discussions throughout the year. Doing this helps to provide a common ground for teachers with the students and thereby increases teacher confidence in discussions about the use of technology in the classrooms. Be careful to provide information to parents. Share examples of student work with different technology applications with the School Council. Ensure that every year one aspect of integrating technology into

The interview with David Dyer that concludes this chapter points to the vital need for educational leaders to convince students to exercise responsibility when using digital technologies.

the classroom is included in the school plan, a plan designed and monitored by administrators and teachers.

Finally, this model can allow you to grow as an educator and as an administrator, leading in a way that will transform your professional practice. Recall our discussion of transformational leadership above. When designing multimodal learning practices, especially as they relate to civic learning, you must be conscious of the strengths and needs of all stakeholders. In this manner, you as the digital principal can open up the potential of the digital world to your students in both safe and dynamic ways.

"It's a Community Effort"

Interview with David Dyer, School Board Officer for Safe and Caring Schools
English District School Board, St. John's, Newfoundland and Labrador

1. How do you promote, model, and establish policies for safe, legal, and ethical use of digital information and technology?

Well, all students in the district must sign and have a parent or guardian sign an online electronics user agreement before accessing school electronics. The district has an acceptable use of information and communication technology policy. With that being said, many students carry their own electronic devices. Schools provide youth with online responsibility and social etiquette information that is regularly discussed within the context of the school day. This information is often provided to parents and guardians so this discussion can continue in the home environment. You know, author Rosalind Wiseman has stated that this technological etiquette standard is the responsibility of society to teach. Parents must become active stakeholders — it is so important that they be included.

2. What about teachers?

Currently, teachers have online guidelines regarding the digital world through the Canadian Teachers' Federation website and NLTA [Newfoundland and Labrador Teachers' Association] articles. A current district policy is in the draft stages for the district — this is intended to help teachers.

3. How do you encourage or promote responsible online social interactions?

All students are provided with education about online learning and responsible engagements through presentations, videos, and discussions. That is a board mandate. We attempt to be as current as possible with these challenges. I have found when talking to students, they rarely comprehend that there is no such thing as privacy when they are online. We try to advise that their online information will be seen and shared by others. Step one.

Most recently, we chose to send out information in the form of a pamphlet. This went home with every child, to make students and parents/guardians aware of the dangers of sexting, which happens outside the school instructional environment.

A teacher's job description is far more than facilitating the curriculum outcomes!

4. What do you emphasize to principals based on what you have experienced?

I have found the majority of youth are responsible with their online social interactions; however, it only takes one message, photo, or video to go viral to shatter an individual, family, or community. The topic needs to become a more engaged conversation with youth. It's a community effort, and our intention is to make it that.

Appendixes

Administrator Technology Profile

1. **In an average week, I use technology for the following purposes for _____ hours:**

(a) Productivity (word processing, presentations)	0	1–5	6–15	16+
(b) Communication (email, Skype, online chat)	0	1–5	6–15	16+
(c) Working with data (spreadsheets, databases)	0	1–5	6–15	16+
(d) Research (Internet browsers)	0	1–5	6–15	16+
(e) Entertainment (games, YouTube)	0	1–5	6–15	16+
(f) Student information/management system	0	1–5	6–15	16+
(g) Professional networking (social media)	0	1–5	6–15	16+
(h) Other (List: _____)	0	1–5	6–15	16+

2. **I would like to improve my ability to do the following with technology:** (Check all that apply.)

   ☐ Use social media to improve communication with staff, parents, students, and the community.
   ☐ Conduct more research via the Internet.
   ☐ Create more documents with word processing and/or databases.
   ☐ Improve the reporting process.
   ☐ Provide better data for decision making.
   ☐ Provide more information about students.
   ☐ Increase communication with colleagues throughout the country.
   ☐ Provide staff development opportunities via the Internet.
   ☐ Improve presentations through the use of multimedia.
   ☐ Change the learning environment throughout the building.

3. **Please complete the following phrase: "My vision concerning the use of technology in education is . . ."**

   _____

   _____

   _____

4. **How valuable do you think the following equipment might be for each classroom in your school?**

	Valuable	Somewhat Valuable	Not So Valuable
Wireless Internet access in each classroom	O	O	O
4 desktop computers in each classroom	O	O	O
4 wireless laptops in each classroom	O	O	O
1 desktop computer for each student in a lab	O	O	O
1 wireless laptop for each student in each classroom	O	O	O
Digital camera for the classroom	O	O	O
1 classroom printer	O	O	O
Multiple classroom printers	O	O	O
TV monitor with VCR	O	O	O
LCD projector/Computer projection system	O	O	O
A tablet for each student	O	O	O

A laptop for teacher use	O	O	O
A tablet for teacher use	O	O	O
Overhead projector	O	O	O
Interactive whiteboard	O	O	O

5. **I would best describe my participation in the development of my board's technology plan as**

   ☐ Not involved   ☐ Not needed: Plan written before I assumed this position
   ☐ Somewhat involved ☐ Very involved

6. **I would best describe my participation in the development of my school's technology plan in this way:** (Circle all that apply.)

   I organized the committee.   I served on the committee.
   I chaired the committee.   Committee worked independently from me.

7. **The following people were encouraged to contribute to the planning process:** (Circle all that apply.)

   Teachers   Students
   Technology facilitators   School board administrators
   Community   Other school staff and administrators
   Parents   Business representatives

8. **How does the technology plan relate to the board's strategic and curriculum implementation plan?** (Mark the one best answer.)

   ☐ There is no technology plan.
   ☐ There is no strategic/curriculum plan.
   ☐ We have both documents, but they are interrelated.
   ☐ The curriculum plan drives the technology plan.
   ☐ The technology plan drives the curriculum plan.
   ☐ The two plans work as one.

9. **How long has it been since the school technology plan was revised?**

   ☐ Being revised now   ☐ Four years
   ☐ One year   ☐ Five years
   ☐ Two years   ☐ More than five years
   ☐ Three years   ☐ Don't know

10. **Briefly describe the process for implementing the school technology plan.**

_____

_____

_____

_____

Pembroke Publishers ©2014 *The Digital Principal* by Janette Hughes, Anne Burke ISBN 9781-55138-288-3

11. **How successfully is the school technology plan being implemented?** (Select one.)

☐ Progress has stalled.
☐ Progress is slow but proceeding.
☐ Implementation is meeting the plan's time lines.
☐ Implementation has been successful and has moved beyond the plan's goals.

12. **If parts of the plan are not working, why do you think they are not working?**

_____

_____

_____

_____

13. **What is the community's attitude towards the use of technology in the school?** (Select one.)

☐ Non-supportive   ☐ Somewhat supportive
☐ Neutral   ☐ Supportive

14. **Generally, what is the staff's attitude towards the use of technology in the school?** (Select one.)

☐ Non-supportive   ☐ Somewhat supportive
☐ Neutral   ☐ Very supportive

15. **How much flexibility do you and other school-level leaders have in determining which types and how much technology is purchased for your school?**

☐ None   ☐ Minimal
☐ Moderate   ☐ Strong

16. **Indicate your degree of agreement with this statement: "With my school, we are currently integrating technology into instructional activities as much as we need to."**

☐ Strongly disagree
☐ Disagree
☐ Neither agree nor disagree
☐ Agree
☐ Strongly agree

17. **What incentives are you using to encourage faculty to participate in technology professional development?** (Check all that apply.)

☐ Tuition reimbursement
☐ Release time
☐ Conference/Seminars/Workshops — expenses covered or reimbursed
☐ Increased technology (e.g., laptop or laptop/projector combo)
☐ Other: _____

Pembroke Publishers ©2014 *The Digital Principal* by Janette Hughes, Anne Burke ISBN 9781-55138-288-3

18. **To what extent do you consider a teacher's instructional use of technology when evaluating a teacher?**
   - ☐ Not considered
   - ☐ Minimal consideration
   - ☐ Important factor

19. **Which professional development opportunities do your teachers use?** (Check all that apply.)
   - ☐ Board workshops
   - ☐ Visits to other schools
   - ☐ On-site vendor presentations
   - ☐ Online courses
   - ☐ Conferences
   - ☐ Peer training and mentoring
   - ☐ Graduate-level university courses
   - ☐ Summer workshops

20. **The following has occurred as a result of technology being available at my school:** (Check all that apply.)
   - ☐ Increased collaborative learning
   - ☐ More individualized curriculum to meet student needs
   - ☐ More class activities that are appropriate for multiple learning styles
   - ☐ Increased use of inquiry-based learning
   - ☐ Increased use of multiple resources in the instructional process
   - ☐ Increased student motivation
   - ☐ Reduced tardiness and absences
   - ☐ Increased creativity in student projects
   - ☐ Increased collaboration among teachers and staff

21. **Rate how much each of these conditions provides obstacles for making effective use of technology in your school:**

	Not an Obstacle	Minor Obstacle	Major Obstacle
There is a lack of computers in the classroom.	O	O	O
Teacher access to computers in labs or library is difficult.	O	O	O
There are not enough computers for all the students.	O	O	O
Professional development prepares teachers to use software not available in my school.	O	O	O
Professional development prepares teachers to use technology in the classroom but does not offer time to practice.	O	O	O
Software is insufficient or inadequate.	O	O	O
Support on how to use technology in the classroom is insufficient or inadequate.	O	O	O
Computers are too unpredictable – they crash or the software does not work properly.	O	O	O
Computers/software available to teachers are outdated.	O	O	O
Increased speed and improved technology negate teachers' previous investments in technology.	O	O	O
Students lack keyboarding skills.	O	O	O
Too many students are in each classroom.	O	O	O

Pembroke Publishers ©2014 *The Digital Principal* by Janette Hughes, Anne Burke ISBN 9781-55138-288-3

The kinds of computers and software at school are different from the computers teachers use at home.	O	O	O
The students lack the skills to use computers effectively.	O	O	O
There is too much course material to cover in a year to make room for technology use.	O	O	O
Teachers lack input into technology decisions.	O	O	O
Teachers have a hard time connecting with the school's technology specialist.	O	O	O
The Internet is too slow.	O	O	O
The computer skills of students vary so widely that it is too difficult to manage computer use.	O	O	O
The academic skills of students vary so widely that computers are not useful in the classroom.	O	O	O

22. **How is software managed?** (Select all that apply.)

☐ Software licences are managed by one person in the building.
☐ Teachers can use only school-purchased software.
☐ Teachers can provide their own software.
☐ Students may bring software and install on school machines.
☐ I don't know.

23. **I use the following set of priorities for purchasing technology when requests exceed budgets.** (Number these according to priority with the item having the highest priority labeled no. 1.)

___ The technology has a direct impact on student learning.
___ The technology enables the teacher to work more effectively.
___ The technology can be used as a part of the curriculum implementation plan.
___ The technology is recommended by the school board.
___ The technology has been requested by a teacher whose work sets an example to follow.
___ The board requires the use of this technology with our students.
___ Technology purchase requests are honored until the budget is exhausted.

24. **I help a teacher who wants to acquire more technology for class projects by**

☐ filling the request if the money is available
☐ asking the teacher to put it in the budget for next year
☐ asking the teacher to purchase it and be reimbursed by the school
☐ encouraging the teacher to find other channels for funding, such as school fundraising
☐ helping the teacher find resources to purchase it
(Check all that apply.)

25. **I help a teacher who is resisting the use of technology by**

_____
_____
_____
_____

26. **The following are examples of technology issues that persist as challenges in my building:**

_____

_____

_____

_____

_____

_____

_____

27. **The following are examples of effective technology implementation in my building:**

_____

_____

_____

_____

_____

_____

Pembroke Publishers ©2014 _The Digital Principal_ by Janette Hughes, Anne Burke ISBN 9781-55138-288-3

Teacher Technology Profile

1. **I have used technology with my students for ___ number of years:** (Circle one.)

   1–5   6–10   11–20   21+

2. **In an average week, I use the following applications for ___ hours:**

(a) Word processing	0	1–5	6–15	16+
(b) Spreadsheets	0	1–5	6–15	16+
(c) Multimedia	0	1–5	6–15	16+
(d) Databases	0	1–5	6–15	16+
(e) Internet	0	1–5	6–15	16+
(f) Simulations	0	1–5	6–15	16+
(g) Reference software	0	1–5	6–15	16+
(h) Drills and practice	0	1–5	6–15	16+
(i) Games	0	1–5	6–15	16+
(j) Drawing	0	1–5	6–15	16+
(k) Desktop publishing	0	1–5	6–15	16+
(l) Photo editing	0	1–5	6–15	16+
(m) Email	0	1–5	6–15	16+
(n) Professional networking	0	1–5	6–15	16+
(o) Social networking	0	1–5	6–15	16+
(p) Chat rooms	0	1–5	6–15	16+
(q) Blogging sites	0	1–5	6–15	16+

3. **What is your comfort level with each of these technology activities?** (Circle one.)

   (a) Producing simple, straightforward learning documents using a word processor
      Not comfortable   1   2   3   4   5   Very comfortable

   (b) Creating educational publications such as parent newsletters and handouts for students
      Not comfortable   1   2   3   4   5   Very comfortable

   (c) Participating in listservs, news groups, and user groups on the Internet
      Not comfortable   1   2   3   4   5   Very comfortable

   (d) Choosing appropriate research tools and applying effective search techniques to produce useful and safe online resources in the classroom
      Not comfortable   1   2   3   4   5   Very comfortable

   (e) Teaching students how to tell the differences between authoritative and untrustworthy sources and how to find sources with different points of view.
      Not comfortable   1   2   3   4   5   Very comfortable

   (f) Having students use technology to do assignments or create projects
      Not comfortable   1   2   3   4   5   Very comfortable

   (g) Organizing and managing email, mobile phones, and text messaging for learning in the classroom
      Not comfortable   1   2   3   4   5   Very comfortable

   (h) Using blogs, wikis, chats, audio and video conferencing to bring outside resources into the classroom and to encourage collaboration among students
      Not comfortable   1   2   3   4   5   Very comfortable

Pembroke Publishers ©2014 *The Digital Principal* by Janette Hughes, Anne Burke ISBN 9781-55138-288-3

(i) Using common tools for preparing slide shows, videos, and podcasts to create presentations that follow the principles of effective communication

Not comfortable   1   2   3   4   5   *Very comfortable*

(j) Incorporating a variety of digital devices into instruction (e.g., Smart Boards, tablets, digital cameras, iPods) and using them to extend learning opportunities

Not comfortable   1   2   3   4   5   *Very comfortable*

4. **Having access to technology in the classroom has helped me to make changes:** (Circle the appropriate choice in each category.)

(a) Students spend more time working together on group projects.
   Minimum or no change   Some change   Significant change

(b) I spend more time coaching or advising students.
   Minimum or no change   Some change   Significant change

(c) I use technology to help integrate curriculum expectations into my teaching.
   Minimum or no change   Some change   Significant change

(d) I let students decide how to use technologies in their projects.
   Minimum or no change   Some change   Significant change

(e) I evaluate electronic versions of student work.
   Minimum or no change   Some change   Significant change

(f) I involve students in the development of learning activities using technology.
   Minimum or no change   Some change   Significant change

(g) I integrate a greater variety of subjects and content into each of my lessons.
   Minimum or no change   Some change   Significant change

5. **How would you classify yourself as a technology user?** (Check one level.)

☐ *Entry:* I am just starting to use technology for learning.

☐ *Adoption:* I have some comfort with technology, and I have taken steps to use it in my teaching.

☐ *Adaptation:* I am moving towards more student-based project learning, and I encourage the use of a variety of technology tools.

☐ *Appropriation:* I am comfortable with technology, and I integrate it throughout most learning activities.

☐ *Transformation:* I often create new ways to use technology tools for real-world applications in my classroom.

6. **How do you want to increase your use of technology?** (Check all that apply.)

☐ Creating documents with word processing

☐ Increasing communication with colleagues in other schools

☐ Using email to communicate with other teachers and staff members within the school

☐ Conducting research via the Internet

☐ Creating multimedia presentations for the class

☐ Designing collaborative projects for my students

☐ Improving classroom record keeping

☐ Designing more curriculum that integrates technology

☐ Individualizing instruction for students

☐ Letting the students use a variety of technology resources to design their own projects

☐ Providing more authentic, real-world activities

☐ Communicating with parents

☐ Using existing digital resources designed for educational purposes in my teaching

☐ Introducing collaborative online learning environments to my students

Pembroke Publishers ©2014 *The Digital Principal* by Janette Hughes, Anne Burke ISBN 9781-55138-288-3

7. **How accessible is the computer lab for your classes?** (Circle the most appropriate response.)

Never   *Once a week*   *2–3 times a week*   *4 times a week*   *Always*

8. **Please respond to the following statements about technology plans.**

   (a) I am aware of my school's technology plans.
   Yes   *No*   *Somewhat*

   (b) I am aware of my board's technology plans.
   Yes   *No*   *Somewhat*

   (c) The plans help define how I use technology in my classroom.
   Yes   *No*   *Somewhat*

   (d) The plans provide guidelines for the purchase of hardware and software.
   Yes   *No*   *Somewhat*

   (e) The plans establish expectations for the use of technology in my classroom.
   Yes   *No*   *Somewhat*

   (f) The plans help establish the integration of technology in curriculum planning.
   Yes   *No*   *Somewhat*

   (g) It is difficult to implement parts of the plans.
   Yes   *No*   *Somewhat*

   (h) I am expected to teach established student technology skills and expectations that have been mandated by the province/state.
   Yes   *No*   *Somewhat*

9. **When you need technology help, where do you go?** (For each possibility, circle one option.)

   (a) My site administrator
   Never   *Sometimes*   *Most of the time*

   (b) Other teachers in my school
   Never   *Sometimes*   *Most of the time*

   (c) My principal or vice-principal
   Never   *Sometimes*   *Most of the time*

   (d) A board facilitator
   Never   *Sometimes*   *Most of the time*

   (e) Students in my class
   Never   *Sometimes*   *Most of the time*

10. **I have learned to use technology through the following methods:** (For each method identified, circle one assessment.)

    (a) By experimenting with the equipment or software — self-taught
    Not a useful method for me   *Secondary method*   *Main method*

    (b) Through board workshops
    Not a useful method for me   *Secondary method*   *Main method*

    (c) By reading manuals
    Not a useful method for me   *Secondary method*   *Main method*

    (d) By attending conferences
    Not a useful method for me   *Secondary method*   *Main method*

    (e) By taking higher education courses
    Not a useful method for me   *Secondary method*   *Main method*

(f) With assistance from peers
   Not a useful method for me   *Secondary method*   *Main method*

(g) Through visits to other schools
   Not a useful method for me   *Secondary method*   *Main method*

11. I have had professional development in technology: (Check all that apply.)

- ☐ Additional Qualification courses
- ☐ Graduate-level university courses
- ☐ Content-area conferences that include technology
- ☐ Technology conferences
- ☐ Board workshops
- ☐ Vendor workshops

12. What would you like to have more training in? (Check all appropriate responses.)

- ☐ Basic computer skills (e.g., accessing programs, printing documents)
- ☐ How to use email (e.g., writing, sending, receiving, storing messages, adding attachments)
- ☐ How to use the Internet (e.g., searches, downloading data, creating and managing Favorites)
- ☐ Specific software programs
- ☐ Software evaluation (e.g., picking the best program for my classroom needs)
- ☐ Technology planning (e.g., how to develop and implement a plan)
- ☐ Technology leadership (e.g., becoming comfortable with decisions related to technology use)
- ☐ Integrating technology into the curriculum (e.g., when and how to use technology)
- ☐ Using technology to teach to various learning styles (e.g., visual, auditory, kinesthetic)
- ☐ Classroom technology management (e.g., managing resources in the classroom)
- ☐ Using technology for assessment

13. Per term, I make assignments in which I expect my students to use technology in the classroom or at home: (Circle the average number of assignments per term.)

(a)	Word processing	0	1	2	3	4+
(b)	Spreadsheet	0	1	2	3	4+
(c)	Multimedia	0	1	2	3	4+
(d)	Database	0	1	2	3	4+
(e)	Internet	0	1	2	3	4+
(f)	Simulations	0	1	2	3	4+
(g)	Reference software	0	1	2	3	4+
(h)	Drill and practice	0	1	2	3	4+
(i)	Games	0	1	2	3	4+
(j)	Drawing	0	1	2	3	4+
(k)	Desktop publishing	0	1	2	3	4+
(l)	Photo editing	0	1	2	3	4+
(m)	Email	0	1	2	3	4+
(n)	Social networking sites	0	1	2	3	4+
(o)	Wikis or blogs	0	1	2	3	4+

Pembroke Publishers ©2014 *The Digital Principal* by Janette Hughes, Anne Burke ISBN 9781-55138-288-3

14. Per term, my students usually use the following software ____ times in the computer lab:
(Circle the average number of assignments per term.)

(a)	Word processing	0	1	2	3	4+
(b)	Spreadsheets	0	1	2	3	4+
(c)	Multimedia	0	1	2	3	4+
(d)	Databases	0	1	2	3	4+
(e)	Internet	0	1	2	3	4+
(f)	Simulations	0	1	2	3	4+
(g)	Reference software	0	1	2	3	4+
(h)	Drills and practice	0	1	2	3	4+
(i)	Games	0	1	2	3	4+
(j)	Drawing	0	1	2	3	4+
(k)	Desktop publishing	0	1	2	3	4+
(l)	Photo editing	0	1	2	3	4+
(m)	Email	0	1	2	3	4+
(n)	Social networking sites	0	1	2	3	4+
(o)	Wikis	0	1	2	3	4+
(p)	Blogs	0	1	2	3	4+

15. In an average week, my students and I devote ____ hours of class time to the following:

(a)	Working in cooperative groups	0	1	2	3	4+
(b)	Independent work time	0	1	2	3	4+
(c)	Organized whole-class discussions	0	1	2	3	4+
(d)	Teacher-delivered material	0	1	2	3	4+
(e)	Presentations by students in the class	0	1	2	3	4+

16. In an average week, my students and I devote class time to the following:

(a) Developing strategies for solving complex problems
Never   Sometimes   Frequently

(b) Developing effective research techniques that use a variety of resources
Never   Sometimes   Frequently

(c) Analyzing and synthesizing information
Never   Sometimes   Frequently

(d) Conducting inquiry-based research
Never   Sometimes   Frequently

(e) Doing activities with authentic, real-life connections
Never   Sometimes   Frequently

(f) Doing activities that involve manipulatives
Never   Sometimes   Frequently

(g) Reflecting on learning
Never   Sometimes   Frequently

Pembroke Publishers ©2014 *The Digital Principal* by Janette Hughes, Anne Burke ISBN 9781-55138-288-3

17. **To what degree has the addition of technology in your classroom resulted in changes in the learning environment?**

(a) Students are physically more active.

    Minimum or no change   *Some change*   *Significant change*

(b) My teaching style has changed.

    Minimum or no change   *Some change*   *Significant change*

(c) The arrangement of the room has been altered to accommodate technology.

    Minimum or no change   *Some change*   *Significant change*

(d) Students are proactive about their own learning.

    Minimum or no change   *Some change*   *Significant change*

(e) Students work together in collaborative groups.

    Minimum or no change   *Some change*   *Significant change*

(f) Student projects involve multimedia.

    Minimum or no change   *Some change*   *Significant change*

(g) Students willingly engage in problem-solving activities.

    Minimum or no change   *Some change*   *Significant change*

(h) Student work is shared with a variety of audiences.

    Minimum or no change   *Some change*   *Significant change*

18. **Briefly describe a lesson that you and your students completed in which the technology worked well.**

_____

_____

_____

_____

_____

_____

Thank you for your participation in this process.

Pembroke Publishers ©2014 *The Digital Principal* by Janette Hughes, Anne Burke ISBN 9781-55138-288-3

Model Unit Plan Using Digital Resources: Cyberbullying

Purpose: To educate students on cyberbullying, how and why it happens, who are the major players, and ways to prevent or stop it.

Rationale: Without proper education on why cyberbullying is both easy and damaging, students may find themselves engaged in it. The anonymity and asynchronous nature of cyberbullying make it a widespread problem among students. As a result, it is necessary for them to understand who is involved in a cyberbullying case, their roles, their reasons for feeling and acting a certain way, and what responsibilities they have in preventing cyberbullying.

Hook: 10 minutes

1. Put students in groups of three or four.
2. Give each group a piece of chart paper with the title "Cyberbullying" and labeled silhouettes or outlines of three people: bully, victim, and bystander
3. Direct them to brainstorm as many words relating to these figures as possible and to record the words within the appropriate outline.

Elaborate: 10 minutes

1. Have the groups share what they came up with, and combine all the commonalities on a board or screen at the front.
2. Ask the groups to use their brainstorming notes to come up with a definition of each major player in cyberbullying. Prompt them to consider what the major players might look like, what they might say or not say, and how they might act. How is each person affected by the experience?
3. Have students compare their answers and discuss.

Learning activities — Avatars and Anonymity: 15 minutes

1. Ask the students what the term *avatar* means. (An *avatar* is a graphical representation of a person's online identity or persona.)
2. Ask them to share the various avatars they may have in their online world (possible places: Facebook, Twitter, Pinterest, Google+, and Instagram).
3. Put the students in pairs. Tell them to create a fictitious character with online and in-person identities that differ either slightly or significantly. More specifically, encourage the students to base their character on a major player in a cyberbullying case: the bully, the victim, or the bystander.
4. Prompt the pairs to create a Venn diagram. Have them list details about the online personality on one side and about the in-person identity on the other side. Tell them to note where the in-person and online identities are the same where the two circles intersect.
5. *Hot seat:* When everyone is finished, explain that the class will be doing a hot-seat activity. Here, each pair will have a turn in the hot seat at the front, and the class will ask them personal questions. One person will respond in character as the online identity and the other, as the in-person identity. Emphasize that students are to respond totally as their character — down to physical posture, tone of voice, and types of responses.

Pembroke Publishers ©2014 *The Digital Principal* by Janette Hughes, Anne Burke ISBN 9781-55138-288-3

6. *Debrief:* Discuss the similarities and differences observed and their significance. What are some affordances and constraints of avatars? Why is it easier to bully someone online than in person? What tools can students use as "self-checkers" before they do something hurtful online?

Inquiry-Based Project Idea

Introduction and explanation

Give the following scenario to your students.
1. Your class is a not-for-profit anti-bullying organization. Since cyberbullying is currently your organization's focus, you are now going to develop public awareness materials to distribute to the immediate and larger communities.
2. You will have seven materials to develop and will be put into the appropriate "departments" in which you will collaborate to develop your assigned material.
3. Further details, examples, and resources will be provided to your department to help you complete your task.
4. For general research, you may visit the following anti-cyberbullying sites:

   http://westophate.org/
   http://www.stopcyberbullying.org/index2.html
   http://kidshealth.org/parent/positive/talk/cyberbullying.html#
   http://www.cyberbullying.org/
   http://www.cnn.com/2013/02/27/health/cyberbullying-online-bully-victims
   http://www.stopbullying.gov/what-is-bullying/index.html
   http://www.americanhumane.org/children/stop-child-abuse/fact-sheets/cyber-bullying-prevention-and-intervention.html
   http://www.adl.org/education-outreach/bullying-cyberbullying/c/strategies-and-resources.html
   http://www.kidshelpphone.ca/teens/infobooth/bullying/cyberbullying.aspx
   http://www.bullyfreealberta.ca/cyber_bullying.htm
   http://antibullying.novascotia.ca/
   http://deal.org/the-knowzone/internet-safety/cyberbullying/

The seven products

1. **One-Minute Public Service Announcement:** Create a one-minute public service announcement focused on one aspect of cyberbullying using a video-editing program such as iMovie or Photo Story.
2. **Office Pamphlet:** Create a pamphlet for visitors to your office to grab. The pamphlet should detail cyberbullying, both direct and by proxy, and what is involved in each.
3. **Print Public Service Announcement:** Focus on the various types of cyberbullies by creating a print ad for billboards and bus stops. Use Glogster or any other poster-making program.
4. **Radio Interview:** Create a five-minute radio interview that could be aired during anti-bullying awareness week. The purpose is to convey why people cyberbully and to identify the different strategies all three players in cyberbullying can use to reduce it. You may use any voice-recorder application you choose — on your phone, tablet, or computer — to record your interview.
5. **Rap or Pop Song:** Create a two- to five-minute rap or pop song on the long-term effects of cyberbullying on both the cyberbully and the victim.

Pembroke Publishers ©2014 *The Digital Principal* by Janette Hughes, Anne Burke ISBN 9781-55138-288-3

6. **Graphic Novella:** Create a 5- to 10-page graphic novella on one student subject to cyberbullying. Use either Comic Life or the online comic-making site, Comic Master.
7. **Website:** Create a Wix or Google website that gives a brief overview of cyberbullying. Consider what categories you will need to use for the navigation menu, and focus on developing at least three of these.

Assessment expectations

Choose and use appropriate curriculum expectations from the ISTE Standards • S and consider local curriculum expectations, too. How well do these align?

Tech-Check: Potential Glitches

Check for the following:

☐ Internet connection
☐ All computers fully powered
☐ Internet browser on all computers working; no restrictions to any of the websites
☐ Projector hooked up and functioning
☐ All website links properly copied and links all working

Computers have the following:

___ video-editing program
___ Comic Life program
___ Microsoft Word or InDesign
___ voice recorders or phones charged and with enough memory

Pembroke Publishers ©2014 *The Digital Principal* by Janette Hughes, Anne Burke ISBN 9781-55138-288-3

Cyberbullying Rubric

Categories	Level 1	Level 2	Level 3	Level 4
Knowledge and Understanding	- demonstrates limited knowledge or understanding of cyberbullying in the material produced	- demonstrates some knowledge or understanding of cyberbullying in the material produced	- demonstrates considerable knowledge or understanding of cyberbullying in the material produced	- demonstrates thorough knowledge or understanding of cyberbullying in the material produced
	- facts and information are incomplete, minimally accurate, or too general	- some facts and information are incomplete, minimally accurate, or too general	- one or two facts or pieces of information are incomplete, minimally accurate, or too general	- facts and information are complete, accurate, and detailed
Thinking	- product does not reflect effective planning, processing, and critical or creative thinking skills with regard to the digital medium or content	- product somewhat reflects effective planning, processing, and critical or creative thinking skills with regard to the digital medium or content	- product considerably reflects effective planning, processing, and critical or creative thinking skills with regard to the digital medium or content	- product thoroughly reflects effective planning, processing, and critical or creative thinking skills with regard to the digital medium and content
	- product is minimally or not aurally and/or visually appealing	- product has some visual and/or aural appeal	- product has considerable visual and/or aural appeal	- product has strong visual and/or aural appeal
	- product has no unique features	-product has some unique features	- product has a considerable amount of unique features	- product has many unique features
Communication	- group expresses and organizes ideas and information with limited effectiveness using their digital medium	- group expresses and organizes ideas and information with some effectiveness using their digital medium	- group expresses and organizes ideas and information with considerable effectiveness using their digital medium	- group thoroughly and effectively expresses and organizes ideas and information using their digital medium
	- technical glitches occur and affect overall presentation	- some technical glitches occur and affect overall presentation	- minor technical glitches occur, but have a minimal impact on overall presentation	- no technical glitches occur

Pembroke Publishers ©2014 *The Digital Principal* by Janette Hughes, Anne Burke ISBN 9781-55138-288-3

Categories	Level 1	Level 2	Level 3	Level 4
Application	- group makes minimal or no effort to use affordances of the digital medium in unexpected ways	- group makes some effort to use affordances of the digital medium in unexpected ways	- group makes a considerable effort to use affordances of the digital medium in unexpected ways	- group makes a thorough effort to use affordances of the digital medium in unexpected ways
	- group makes minimal or weak connections to relevant experiences or real-life situations	- group makes some connections to relevant experiences or real-life situations	- group makes considerable connections to relevant experiences or real-life situations	- group makes thorough connections to relevant experiences or real-life situations

Pembroke Publishers ©2014 *The Digital Principal* by Janette Hughes, Anne Burke ISBN 9781-55138-288-3

References

Banaji, S., & Burn, A. (2008). *Rhetorics of creativity* (2nd ed.). London, England: Arts Council. Retrieved from http://www.creativitycultureeducation.org/wp-content/uploads/rhetorics-of-creativity-2nd-edition-87.pdf

Bass, B. M., & Avolio, B. J. (1994). *Improving organizational effectiveness through transformational leadership.* Thousand Oaks, CA: Sage.

Bearne, E., Ellis, S., Graham, L., Hulme, P., Meiner, J., & Wolstencroft, H. (2005). *More than words 2: Creating stories on page and screen.* London, England: Qualifications and Curriculum Authority; Royston, England: United Kingdom Literacy Association. Retrieved from http://labspace.open.ac.uk/file.php/8252/1847210724.pdf

Bearne, E. (2009). Assessing multimodal texts. In A. Burke & R. F. Hammett (Eds.), *Assessing new literacies: Perspectives from the classroom* (pp. 15–33). New York, NY: Peter Lang.

Beetham, H., McGill, L., & Littlejohn, A. (2009). *Thriving in the 21st century: Report of the Learning Literacies in a Digital Age Project.* London, England: Jisc.

Burke, A. (2012). Authoring of self: Identity and family cultural practices. In K. James, T. M. Dobson, & C. Leggo (Eds.), *English in middle and secondary classrooms: Creative and critical advice from Canada's teacher educators* (pp. 1–29). Toronto, ON: Pearson Education.

Burke, A. (2013). Creating identity: The online worlds of two English language learners. *Language and Literacy: A Canadian Educational E-journal, 15*(3), 31–49.

Burke, A., Butland, L., & Roberts, K. l. (2013). Using multiliteracies to rethink literacy pedagogy in elementary classrooms. *Journal of Technology Integration in the Classroom, 1*(2), 16–38.

Burke, A., Hughes, J., Hardware, S., & Thompson, S. (2013). Adolescents as agents of change: Digital text-making for social justice. *Education Matters, 1*(2). Retrieved from http://em.synergiesprairies.ca/index.php/em/article/view/45/20

Burke, A., & Marsh, J. (2013). *Children's virtual playworlds: Culture, learning and participation.* New York, NY: Peter Lang.

Canada Safety Council. (2012). Cyberbullying. Retrieved from https://canadasafetycouncil.org/child-safety/cyber-bullying

Canadian Council on Learning. (2009). *Post-secondary Education in Canada: Meeting Our Needs?* Ottawa, ON: Author. Retrieved from www.ccl-cca.ca

Canadian Teachers' Federation [CTF]. (2011). The Copyright Modernization Act: A Canadian Teachers' Federation brief to the Legislative Committee on Bill C-32, *an Act to amend the Copyright Act.* Retrieved from http://www.ctf-fce.ca/Research-Library/Brief_Copyright2010-11.pdf

City of Toronto. (2006). West Hill neighbourhood profile. Retrieved from http://www.toronto.ca/demographics/cns_profiles/cns136.htm

Centre for Innovative & Entrepreneurial Leadership [CIEL]. Communities Life Cycle Matrix, Version 1.3. Retrieved from http://www.theciel.com/documents/CommunitiesMatrix.pdf

Cradler, J., McNabb, M., Freeman, M., & Burchett, R. (2002). How does technology influence student learning? *Learning and Leading with Technology, 29*(8), 46–49, 56. Retrieved from http://www.lakeridge.k12.in.us/cms/lib7/IN01000416/Centricity/Domain/205/techology%20influence.pdf

Darling-Hammond, L. (2010). New policies for 21st century demands. In J. Bellanca & R. Brandt (Eds.), *21st century skills: Rethinking how students learn* (pp. 33–50). Bloomington, IN: Solution Tree Press.

Davison, J. (2013). Can cyberbullying laws really work? *CBC News.* Retrieved from http://www.cbc.ca/news/canada/can-cyberbullying-laws-really-work-1.1367611

DuFour, R. (2004, May). What is a professional learning community? *Educational Leadership, 61*(8), 6–11.

DuFour, R., & Mattos, M. (2013). How do principals really improve schools? *Educational Leadership, 70*(7), 34–40. Retrieved from http://www.ascd.org/publications/educational-leadership/apr13/vol70/num07/How-Do-Principals-Really-Improve-Schools%C2%A2.aspx

Earle, R. S. (2002). The integration of instructional technology into public education: Promises and challenges. *Educational Technology, 42*(1), 5–13.

Edelson, D., Gordin, D., & Pea, R. (1999). Addressing the challenges of inquiry-based learning through technology and curriculum design. *Journal of the Learning Sciences, 8*(3 & 4), 391–450.

Franciosi, S. J. (2012). Transformational leadership for education in a digital culture. *Digital Culture and Education, 4*(1). Retrieved from http://www.digitalcultureandeducation.com/volume-4/transformational-leadership-for-education-in-a-digital-culture/

Fullan, M. G. (1993). Why teachers must become change agents. *Educational Leadership, 50*, 12–17.

Fullan, M. G., & Miles, M. B. (1992). Getting reform right: What works and what doesn't. *Phi Delta Kappan, 73*, 745–752.

Fullan, M., & Quinn, J. (2012). *Leading transformational change.* Washington, DC: International Society for Technology in Education (ISTE).

Gee, J. (2004). *Situated language and learning: A critique of traditional schooling.* New York, NY: Routledge.

Herbert, M. (2010, November). The iPad — Breaking new ground in Special Education. *District Administration: Solutions for School District Management.* Retrieved from http://www.districtadministration.com/article/ipad%E2%80%94breaking-new-ground-special-education

Hughes, J. (2009). New media, new literacies & the adolescent learner [Special issue]. *E-Learning and Digital Media, 6*(3), 259–271.

Hughes, J., & Burke, A. (2012). Using ICTs in middle school literacy programs. In A. Mendez-Vilas (Ed.), *Education in a technological world: Communicating current and emerging research and technological efforts* (pp. 581–587). Badajoz, Spain: Formatex.

Hughes, J., & Morrison, L. (2013). Facebook to explore adolescence identities [Special issue]. *International Journal of Social Media and Interactive Learning Environments, 1*(4), 370–386.

Hughes, J., & Thompson, S. (2013). ImMEDIAte gratification: Examining the use of mobile devices in adolescents' in-school and out-of-school lives [Special issue]. *Learning Landscapes, 6*(2), 185–205.

Hughes, J., Thompson, S., & Burke, A. (2013). The writing is on my wall: Engagements and LearNING through Social Networking. *The International Journal of Technologies in Learning, 19*(3), 107–118.

Hughes, J., & Tolley, S. (2010). Engaging students through new literacies: The good, bad & curriculum of visual essays. *English in Education, 44*(1), 5–16.

Hutchison, A., & Reinking, D. (2011). Teachers' perceptions of integrating information and communication technologies into literacy instruction: A national survey in the United States. *Reading Research Quarterly, 46*, 312–333.

International Society for Technology in Education [ISTE]. Essential conditions: Necessary conditions to effectively leverage technology for learning. Retrieved from http://www.iste.org/docs/pdfs/netsessentialconditions.pdf?sfvrsn=2

International Society for Technology in Education [ISTE]. Standards for administrators. Retrieved from https://www.iste.org/standards/standards-for-administrators

International Society for Technology in Education [ISTE]. Standards for students. Retrieved from https://www.iste.org/standards/standards-for-students

International Society for Technology in Education [ISTE]. Standards for teachers. Retrieved from https://www.iste.org/standards/standards-for-teachers

Jenkins, L. (2012). Reversing the downslide of student enthusiasm. *School Administrator, 5*(69), 16–17.

Jewitt, C. (2003, March). Re-thinking assessment: Multimodality, literacy and computer-mediated learning. *Assessment in Education, 10*(1), 83–102.

Jewitt, C. (2006). *Technology, literacy, and learning: A multimodal approach.* New York, NY: Routledge.

Jones, R., & Hafner, C. (2012). *Understanding digital literacies: A practical introduction.* New York, NY: Routledge.

Kennewell, S. (2001). Using affordances and constraints to evaluate the use of information and communications technology in teaching and learning. *Journal of Information Technology for Teacher Education, 10*(1–2), 101–116.

Leithwood, K. A. (1992). The move toward transformational leadership. *Educational Leadership, 49*(5), 8–12.

Leithwood, K., & Jantzi, D. (1991). Transformational leadership: How principals can help reform school cultures. *School Effectiveness and School Improvement, 1*(3), 249–281.

Loveless, A. (2007). *Creativity, technology and learning.* Bristol, England: Futurelab.

Marzano, R. J. (2011, February). The art & science of teaching: Making the most of instructional rounds. *Instructional Leadership, 60*(5), 80–82.

Martin, J. The 6th grade program of St. Greg's digital citizenship bootcamp. Retrieved from http://21k12blog.net/2011/09/12/the-6th-grade-program-of-st-gregs-digital-citizenship-bootcamp/

McClay, J. K., & Mackey, M. (2009). Distributed assessment in OurSpace: This is not a rubric. In A. Burke & R. F. Hammet (Eds.), *Assessing new literacies: Perspectives from the classroom* (pp. 113–132). New York, NY: Peter Lang Publishing.

New London Group. (1996). A pedagogy of multiliteracies: Designing social futures. *Harvard Educational Review, 66*(1), 60–92.

O'Hara, S., & Pritchard, R. (2010). What is the impact of technology on learning? Retrieved from Education.com website: http://www.education.com/reference/article/what-impact-technology-learning/

Ontario Ministry of Education. (2010). *Student success — Differentiated instruction educator's package.* Toronto, ON: Queen's Printer for Ontario.

Peel District School Board. (2012). *Vision for 21st century teaching and learning.* Retrieved from http://www.peelschools.org/aboutus/21stCentury/byod/parentresources/Documents/Vision%20for%2021st%20Century%20Teaching%20and%20Learning.pdf

Prensky, M. (2005, September/October). "Engage me or enrage me": What today's learners demand. *Educause Review, 40*(5), 60–64.

Raywid, M. A. (1993). Finding time for collaboration. *Educational Leadership, 51*(1), 30–34.

Reigeluth, C., & Karnopp, J. (2013). *Reinventing schools: It's time to break the mold.* New York, NY: Rowman & Littlefield.

Richardson, W., & Mancabelli, R. (2011). *Personal learning networks: Using the power of connections to transform education.* Bloomington, IN: Solution Tree Press.

Rogers, E. M. (2003). *Diffusion of innovations* (5th ed.). New York, NY: Free Press.

Rose, D., Meyer, A., Strangman, N., & Rappolt, G. (2002). *Teaching every student in the digital age.* Alexandria, VA: ASCD.

Salmon, G. (2005). *E-moderating: The key to teaching and learning online.* New York, NY: RoutledgeFalmer.

Schaps, E. (2003). Creating a school community. *Educational Leadership, 60*(6), 31–33.

Selber, S. (2004). *Multiliteracies for a digital age.* Carbondale, IL: Southern Illinois University Press.

Senge, P. (1990). *The fifth discipline: The art and practice of the learning organization.* New York, NY: Doubleday.

Sherry, L., & Gibson, D. (2002). The path to teacher leadership in educational technology. *Contemporary Issues in Technology and Teacher Education, 2*(2), 178–203.

Sivin-Kachala, J., & Bialo, E. (2000). *2000 research report on the effectiveness of technology in schools* (7th ed.). Washington, DC: Software & Information Industry Association [SIIA].

Tomlinson, C. A., & Allan, S. D. (2000). *Leadership for differentiating schools and classrooms.* Alexandria, VA: Association for Supervision and Curriculum Development.

Underwood, J. (2009). *The impact of digital technology: A review of the evidence of the impact of digital technologies on formal education.* Coventry, England: Becta.

Wenger, E. (1998). *Communities of practice: Learning, meaning and identity.* Boston, MA: Cambridge University Press.

Wenger, E. (2000). Communities of practice and social learning systems. *Organization, 7*(2), 225–246.

Wenger, E. (2007). *Communities of practice. A brief introduction.* Retrieved from http://www.ewenger.com/theory/index.htm

World Intellectual Property Organization. (n.d.). Definition of intellectual property. Retrieved from http://www.wipo.int/about-ip/en/

Wyatt-Smith, C., & Kimber, K. (2009). Working multimodally: Challenges for assessment. *English Teaching: Practice and Critique, 8*(3), 70–90.

Index